UNBREAKABLE
WINGS

PILOTING THE IMPOSSIBLE JOURNEY
THROUGH CANCER AND NAVAL AVIATION

CAPT DEREK ADAMETZ, USN (RET.)

Ballast Books, LLC
www.ballastbooks.com

Copyright © 2025 by Derek Adametz

The views expressed in this publication are those of the author and do not necessarily reflect the official policy or position of the Department of Defense or the U.S. government. The public release clearance of this publication by the Department of Defense does not imply Department of Defense endorsement or factual accuracy of the material.

ISBN:
Hardcover: 978-1-966786-27-6
Paperback: 978-1-966786-28-3
Ebook: 978-1-966786-29-0

Printed in the United States of America

Published by Ballast Books
www.ballastbooks.com

For more information, bulk orders, appearances, or speaking requests, please email: info@ballastbooks.com

For the dreamers and fighters—
May you find strength in your scars,
courage in your chaos,
and a little light within these pages.

TABLE OF CONTENTS

PROLOGUE

Life is a relentless journey filled with turbulence and unexpected twists. Its unpredictability is unsettling, shaking even the strongest foundation. Within that uncertainty lies a truth that I have yet to discover. Adversity carves out individuality, forging resilience in the face of impossible odds. Every choice, every moment of hesitation or courage, alters the course of not just my life but countless others, like ripples spreading across an endless sea.

But what happens when the spirit falters? When hope collapses beneath the weight of disappointment so profound that it drains the soul of all feeling? There comes a moment when setbacks press so heavily that numbness seems like the only refuge. Surrendering to the void is so much easier than enduring the torture of unmet expectations. Within that emptiness lies a choice: Remain adrift or fight. What will it take to reclaim what was lost, to rise, and to soar once more?

Confined to the suffocating silence of a darkened hospital room, beyond the reach of divine solace, I lie alone. Everything I have ever known, everything I have ever been, has come to an unnerving halt. Abandoned by certainty, I am imprisoned in my own mind, forsaken by my thoughts, and contemplating how I will leave this room. As I struggle to understand what lies ahead, I will soon come to understand that this is only the beginning of an impossible journey.

CHAPTER I

It was the summer of 1980-something when my dad started a new job, setting in motion a move that would uproot our family from the quiet familiarity of Wautoma, Wisconsin, to the village of McFarland, Wisconsin, located just a few miles south of Madison. For my dad, it was an opportunity, perhaps a fresh start, but for me, it was a daunting leap into the unknown. The prospect of spending the summer in an unfamiliar "village," far from the friends and places I had always known, filled me with worry. And come fall, I would be starting at a new elementary school where I knew no one. The thought of making new friends and finding my place in an unfamiliar world felt almost impossible at that age.

I was incredibly close with my dad. He was of average height with thick, dark hair and, by all accounts, a strikingly handsome man. He had a passion for country line dancing and spent countless hours riding and training horses with his brothers. When I wasn't in school, I spent nearly all my free time by his side. Summer nights and weekends meant casting fishing lines from the back of our classic 1973 fifteen-foot Glastron boat on Lake Waubesa, drifting lazily with the current as we reeled in fish and joked over who'd caught more.

When we weren't fishing, I was mastering the art of waterskiing, cutting across the water and jumping the boat's wake, or learning to drive the boat under my dad's watchful eye. When fall arrived and temperatures dropped, our weekends belonged to the family dairy farm in Montfort, Wisconsin, where hunting and spending time with relatives filled our days. And, of course, no visit was complete without me getting roped into farm chores, where uncles taught me valuable life lessons that every young boy should know, along with a few choice swear words.

Amid Wisconsin's brutal winters, Dad and I would lace up our skates at Lewis Park, where I learned to play hockey and discovered why hot chocolate always tasted better after hours in the cold. When I wasn't on the ice, wobbling to keep balance, I was outside at home, bundled up against the frigid wind and cold. My 1980s winter Moon Boots kept my toes toasty warm as I played in the snow. The yard, an endless blanket of white, became my playground of possibility. I built tunnels, dug forts from towering snowdrifts, and sculpted whatever my imagination dreamed up.

With the unlimited winter fun came the inevitable trade-off, namely shoveling the driveway. Just as I had finished clearing the driveway, my back aching from heaving snow to the outer edges, I would hear the distant rumble of the snowplow. Bracing for the inescapable, I would stand in the driveway, shaking my fist in frustration as it barreled past, leaving behind a fresh, impenetrable mound of packed snow and frozen slush. The mound was often taller than me, and I would spend what felt like hours clearing it so Dad could actually pull into the driveway when he returned from work.

Then there was the mailbox, another battle in the war against winter. Not only did I have to dig it out of the snowbank, but I also had to carve out enough space for the mailman to reach it, a thankless task for a kid who rarely received mail in the first place.

Although McFarland was my hometown, I was raised on our family farm, where I learned life's most valuable lessons and the true meaning of hard work. Every hay bale stacked, every cow milked, and every animal fed reinforced my sense of responsibility and built the foundation of my work ethic. Long days alongside my dad, immersed in the hands-on experiences of farm life, shaped the person I am today.

Work and life were inseparable. Hard work wasn't just encouraged; it was expected. There was no slipping away or making excuses when a full wagon rolled into the driveway. It was a collective effort, a shared commitment to keeping the farm running, so everyone pulled their weight, no questions asked.

The farm offered a kind of fun and adventure that life in McFarland simply couldn't match. The barn, surrounding buildings, and endless fields of tall green stalks of corn became our playground. Towering stacks of hay begged to be climbed, with hidden tunnels to crawl through. The rows of corn beckoned us to run as fast as we could, weaving between them as we chased after each other. Silos stood like cement giants, their ladders daring us to scale them, and BB guns provided endless entertainment, especially with the farm's ever-growing pigeon population as challenging targets. With cousins by my side, I spent hours exploring every building, every field, and every pasture, each one brimming with the promise of adventure.

Harvest season proved to be busy, and I spent entire summer days driving an old Oliver tractor, pulling an even older New Holland rake, carefully turning over recently cut hay in every field to ensure it dried thoroughly before baling. Hours passed to the steady hum of the engine, the clicking of the rake as it spun behind me, and the muffler billowing thick black smoke straight into my face. The refreshing scents of tractor exhaust and earthy sweet-cut hay occupied my mind for hours.

By the time the sun dipped toward the horizon, my face was dark with diesel exhaust and a day's worth of dust from raking an entire field—or three. I secured the rake for road travel, climbed back onto the tractor, and headed to the farm. The irony after returning from an exhausting day in the field was the reward of more work and finishing the day's chores.

No matter how weary I was, a small surprise always awaited me as I turned onto the long gravel driveway. The farm's cow dogs roamed loose on the grounds and were always there to greet anyone who dared enter. Barking excitedly, they ran alongside, announcing my arrival as if to protect the farm. They followed me all the way until I parked; their energetic welcome made it nearly impossible to step off the tractor. And before I could move on to the next task, each of them demanded well-earned pets and attention for keeping the farm safe from intruders. Fierce protector dogs they were not, but loyal companions they certainly were.

After spending most of the day on a tractor seat, the walk down to the barn for evening milking was a chance to stretch my legs, loosen my back, and shake the dust from my clothes. To anyone watching from a distance, it probably just looked like I was swatting at invisible bugs or randomly slapping myself. On my quick stop in the milkhouse, I welcomed the sight of the garden hose affixed to the wall faucet. It was our main source of drinking water, and it was always cold, refreshing, and exactly what I needed before heading into the barn to help milk the cows.

As milking wrapped up, my final task of the day was filling bottles with milk to feed the young calves, a job that felt more like a lesson in cage wrestling. Overexcited for feeding time, they would nudge, bump, and shove against me, their soaking wet, milky, slobber-covered heads smearing across my arms and clothes as they eagerly searched for more. The trick was to keep my back up against the wall inside their pen while holding the bottles, unless I wanted an adventurous calf to land a solid nudge to my backside.

Chores became easier by the time I reached middle school, and my curiosity for how things worked had deepened. I found myself drawn to the shed or garage, eager to gain further knowledge. Whether on the farm or at home, I'd spend my free time disassembling and reassembling bicycles and anything else mechanical I could find, using tools to cut, drill, and fasten scrap wood or items together. I dove into any hands-on project that kept my mind and body engaged. The farm fueled my curiosity and interest, with machinery always in some stage of repair or disassembly. Grandpa was constantly welding farm equipment, and Dad was always fixing something at home. Watching them work, I realized that every challenge held a lesson and that no problem was insurmountable with the right tools and the determination to solve it.

Dad earned the nickname "Do-It-Twice-Steve" because every repair he attempted seemed to require a second try after something inevitably went wrong the first time. My job was to hold the flashlight, which mostly meant getting yelled at whenever I wasn't pointing it exactly where he wanted. At the time, I felt bad about it, but looking back, I realize he wasn't really mad at me. His frustration stemmed from having to redo the job, and he needed someone to vent to. As the designated flashlight holder, that someone was usually me.

I grew up fast on the farm. One day, around the age of twelve, I was out in the field on a typical hot and humid afternoon when Grandpa pulled up in his truck and waved me down. I shut off the tractor and walked over to see what he needed. "Hop in," he said, and we drove to the adjacent field where he was baling the hay I had raked a few days earlier. Without hesitation, he tossed me the keys and told me to hook up to the wagon stacked with hay bales, drive it five miles back to the farm, unload it, and return with the empty wagon so he could keep baling. I had driven trucks on the farm, on back roads, and in the fields, but this was my first time driving on a main road, and pulling a full wagonload of hay made it even more nerve-wracking. But there was no question; I had a job to do, and I wasn't about to let Grandpa down. In that moment, panic set in as I drove out of the field and onto the paved highway, careful not to turn too sharply and tip the wagon into the ditch. Looking back, I realize that moment was exactly what I needed to build confidence in myself and press forward without hesitation.

Transferring hay bales from the wagon to the barn was deceptively simple yet far more grueling in practice. The bales, scattered and packed tightly into the wagon during baling, had to be unloaded one by one, a process that demanded both strength and endurance. Ideally, many hands would share the workload, making the job less punishing, but more often than not, there were only a few of us, and on some occasions, just two of us. My uncle usually unloaded the wagon, gripping each dense, scratchy bale and wrestling it free from the tangled heap before heaving it onto the conveyor. The conveyor groaned and rattled as it carried it up a long ramp, through a square cutout hole in the side of the barn, and into the dim, sweltering haymow. At the top, the bales tumbled off the end of the conveyor in an explosion of dry chaff and dust, filling the air with a golden, shimmery haze. The itchy debris clung to my sweaty skin, worked its way down the back of my shirt, filled my nose, covered my hat and hair, and even found its way into my pants pockets.

Finally old enough to work the haymow on my own, I could survive as long as the bales moved up the conveyor at a steady, manageable pace. The intense heat and the heavy weight of the bales were bearable, but stacking them demanded an engineer's eye. In theory, the bales should have fit together neatly, like a puzzle of similar rectangular pieces. In reality, they were more banana-shaped, creating an uneven surface with hidden gaps that only revealed themselves when I inevitably stepped into one, all while bales continued to tumble from the conveyor, stacking up like an angry pyramid.

I spent the next few summers working on the farm as my summer job, earning a weekly salary from Grandpa in exchange for becoming a more integral part of the daily routine and summer harvest. Instead of just pitching in with chores and fieldwork, I was now getting paid and given more autonomy and responsibility. Instead of just tagging along with an uncle for chores, I was now driving trucks and operating machinery on my own. With each season, I gained more experience and confidence, feeling a greater sense of duty.

The excitement I'd once felt for farm chores gradually faded with age, replaced by the steady, relentless grind of daily tasks. I quickly learned that farm work never paused; there were no vacations, no days off. Time was measured by the unwavering precision of feeding schedules and the twice-daily milking of the cows. The pigs, impatient and unruly, erupted in fury if their meals were even slightly delayed. Their loud grunts and ear-piercing squeals carried an ominous intensity, far removed from the cute and playful "oink" we all imagine. This demanding routine was difficult but instilled a strong work ethic, where every task, no matter how small, demanded attention and discipline. The farm didn't just teach me how to work hard; it taught responsibility, resilience, and the importance of being dependable, day in and day out.

With the passing of each school year, I found myself living two separate lives. During the week in McFarland, I had a paper route, spent time with friends, and enjoyed the typical school routine. But on weekends, I stepped into farm life, transforming into someone entirely different. Grandpa often teased me, calling me a "city slicker," and I couldn't deny there was some truth to it. Yet nearly every weekend up through junior high, Dad and I would head to the farm, immersing ourselves in the sights, sounds, and unmistakable smells that made it unforgettable. The contrast between these two lives was striking, yet I felt at home in both.

Then, for the first time, tragedy struck. It was a spring day, and we were outside for gym class learning tennis. The school had a machine that launched balls autonomously, and we took turns practicing our swings while the rest of the class gathered loose balls from around the court and refilled the machine. As the period wound down, I bent to pick up a stray ball behind the machine. Just as I stood up, a returned shot struck me squarely in my left eye. In hindsight, we probably should have been wearing eye protection, but it was the 1980s, and safety precautions weren't exactly a priority back then.

The vision in my left eye deteriorated throughout the day, and my iris darkened in color from hazel to deep purple. I was worried but too embarrassed to make a big deal about being hit by a tennis ball, so I kept quiet. But then, while buying candy with friends after school, I ran into my neighbor, who just happened to be a nurse. She stopped to say hello and chat, immediately noticing my eye. When I explained what had happened, she didn't hesitate. Without a second thought, she gave me a ride home and urged my parents to take me to an eye doctor immediately.

The eye doctor ran a series of tests and diagnosed me with a hyphema, a condition where blood pools in the back of the eye due to injury. He expressed concern about potential complications and decided to admit me to the hospital. I'd had more than my share of cuts, bruises, and stitches from my time on the farm, but that was my first time being hospitalized for an injury, so I was nervous. After changing into comfortable clothes, I tried to settle into the hospital bed, doing my best to stay calm. A nurse came into the room and explained that both of my eyes needed to be covered to prevent any movement in one eye from triggering movement in the other, which could worsen my condition.

On top of that, I had to take a large pill every four hours to help reduce inflammation.

Barely a teenager, I sat completely alone and blind in a hospital room, confined to one spot for seven long, agonizing days. Without sight, I lost all sense of time, as days were just as dark and endless as the nights. Seven days were really 168 continuous hours. My only marker of time passing came from brief interactions with the nurse when I needed to use the restroom, eat, or take my pill, marking the slow progression of my isolation.

That was my first true test of patience and resilience. A young kid bursting with energy, the sheer stillness of being trapped in darkness, whether my eyes were open or closed, was an experience I never could have prepared for. Now that I was deprived of sight, my thoughts grew louder, and the silence of the room was deafening. Waves of panic crept in, my mind racing with uncertainty, thinking through all the possible long-term effects. The doctor had spoken mostly with my parents, leaving me with little understanding of the situation. The fear of the unknown gnawed at me, and I had no choice but to take control of my thoughts and find the strength to overcome the silence.

When the time finally came to remove the eye patches, even the faintest light filtering through the curtains in an otherwise dark room was overwhelming. My eyes struggled to adjust, unable to focus on anything with clarity. Instinctively, I kept closing them, seeking comfort in the darkness I had grown accustomed to. The doctor was pleased with the results and cleared me for discharge. With no planned follow-up treatment or tests, I hesitantly left the hospital and returned to school just in time for the final few weeks of class, faced with the task of catching up on homework and missed exams before the end of the school year.

It was May 1986, and Dad wanted to do something special for my birthday, especially since I was still reeling from my eye injury and the mental challenges I had faced in the hospital. He took me to the mall, where we browsed through the aisles of fishing gear, water skis, and hunting equipment, things that reminded me of the outdoor freedom I had been missing. After that, we headed to the arcade, my ultimate hangout spot in the eighties. The bright lights and chorus of familiar beeping and buzzing sounds from the video games and the clatter of tokens dropping from the change machine felt like a much-needed escape from everything I had been through. For the first time in weeks, I wasn't thinking about the terror of the hospital room; I was just a kid again, lost in the thrill of video games.

After we ran out of tokens, Dad suggested we catch a movie, especially since the theater entrance was conveniently across from the arcade. I had always loved going to the movies. There was something magical about it, an experience larger than life. The massive screen and incredible sound were a world away from our old twenty-five-inch Zenith cabinet TV with its fuzzy screen and mono speaker. I was excited at the idea of sitting in a dark theater, surrounded by the scent of buttered popcorn and the quiet anticipation of the audience. It felt like a thrilling escape, and I couldn't wait to immerse myself in another cinematic adventure.

We stood in line, and as I gazed up at the glowing marquee to see what was playing, it was clear that *Short Circuit* was the movie to see. The movie trailer had completely captured my imagination, featuring Number 5, a robot struck by lightning, suddenly alive, curious, and transforming into Johnny 5. When I shared my excitement with Dad, he suggested that *Top Gun* might be a better choice.

I wasn't convinced and put up a fight. I was reluctant to see a movie about airplanes. I was here for Johnny 5 and his adventures, not jets and love stories. I pleaded my case, but Dad held firm. As we stepped up to the counter, Dad asked for one adult and one child for *Top Gun*. Disappointed, I shuffled into the theater, unaware that this moment and his decision would change my life forever.

From the very opening scene, the music captivated me, and I was hooked. The roar of the jet engines, the heart-pounding sound, and the intensity when the words "TOP GUN" appeared on the screen. By the time Dad and I walked out of the theater, *Short Circuit* was a distant memory.

I had always found flying fascinating. Dad flew remote-controlled airplanes, and I was mesmerized watching crop dusters skim low over the fields on the farm. But until that day, I had never given much thought to what I wanted to be when I grew up. Aside from my experiences on the farm, the future had always felt distant and undefined.

While we were driving home from such an incredible day, my mind kept drifting back to the film. The intensity, sounds, speed, and adrenaline all seemed exhilarating. For the first time, I found myself dreaming about the possibility of becoming a pilot.

When junior high ended, so did much of the cherished time I had spent with my dad. Though I remained close to my family, the demands of high school pulled me away from the farm and into a whirlwind of classes, sports, social events, and activities. Stepping into this new world as one of the largest and heaviest kids in the freshman class, I quickly became a target for ridicule, not just from my peers but from upperclassmen as well. The sting of their taunts only compounded the challenges of an already-difficult transition, making high school feel less like an exciting new chapter and more like a hostile environment.

Navigating the social awkwardness of freshman year, I relied heavily on my well-honed skills of humor and sarcasm. Traits I'd clearly picked up from farm life, where entertaining banter and sharp wit were as essential as a good pair of work boots. Fortunately, I was smart enough to surround myself with more popular friends, keeping me loosely tethered to the mainstream by association. Meanwhile, the relentless work ethic I'd cultivated on the farm seamlessly transferred to the classroom. I paid attention and studied when I needed to, and my grades landed me near the top of my class. An achievement that, ironically, only distanced me further from the popular crowd. Turns out, excelling at school wasn't exactly the golden ticket to social stardom.

When it came to athletics, my dairy product-fueled farm physique made me an ideal candidate for the football team's defensive line, especially since I'd played well in junior high. I was all set to play football my freshman year when a friend convinced me to join the cross-country team instead. Naturally, as the biggest kid on the junior varsity team, I was the runner who finished well behind everyone else. I vividly remember one of my earliest races when the race organizers began packing up the finish line and equipment while I was still out on the course. As I neared the finish line, which was being disassembled, I could hear the pity claps from the crowd, accompanied by the encouraging but slightly condescending shouts of "Great job!" and "Way to go!" and "Keep it up!"

I was embarrassed, but I didn't give up. During the off-season, I put in the work, ran every day on my own, and shed the extra weight. I made the varsity team by my junior year and had the greatest coach, one who never gave up on me. He taught me the fundamentals of fitness and running in such a clear and concise way that I still apply his lessons to exercise today. He was strict, set high expectations, and never hesitated to show his disappointment when I didn't put in the effort to achieve my goals. His guidance shaped not only my athletic journey but also my work ethic and discipline. He was and will always be an inspiration to me and everyone he coached.

The fashion style of the late eighties, bursting with energy and personality, was impossible to ignore. I embraced the era wholeheartedly, sporting a classic mullet hairstyle, stone-washed jeans cupped at the bottom, and an array of bright neon colors that reflected the vibrant spirit of the time. My school pictures serve as a time capsule, showcasing brands like Bugle Boy and Z. Cavaricci alongside the influence of hair metal music and a touch of youthful rebellion. Each snapshot is a vivid reminder of a decade defined by bold choices and unforgettable trends.

My sixteenth birthday approached, and I was very excited about getting a vehicle of my own. I had been driving for a few years on the farm and really wanted a manual stick shift for my first vehicle. I had a decent amount of money saved, but I knew I needed to be smart about it, setting some aside for gas and inevitable repairs. Having grown up driving trucks, I never even considered a car; a truck just made sense. I was accustomed to a lifestyle where the bed of a truck was an essential tool in everyday life. Plus, with college on the horizon in a few years, I needed something to help carry and transport all my belongings for moving in and out.

Weekends were spent visiting local dealerships and private sellers, test-driving trucks in search of the perfect vehicle. Options were limited in my price range, and most of the trucks we found bore the unmistakable mark of Wisconsin winters, with rust eating away at the fenders and bed. Then, late one night, we stumbled upon a 1981 brown Toyota pickup with a light beige topper. It had some rust in the bed, but overall, it was in great shape and drove well.

Dad was a haggler, always ready for the opportunity to negotiate, and wasn't about to let that deal slip away without a fight. After what felt like hours of back-and-forth over every last dollar, the night wore on, and I was ready to call it quits and focus on school in the morning. But just as we reached the door, the salesman came rushing after us, finally conceding to Dad's desired price. That night, with an overwhelming sense of pride and excitement, I drove home in my first truck, a moment I would never forget.

Senior year appeared suddenly, and thoughts of college and what I wanted to be when I grew up occupied my thoughts. My interest in mechanical equipment and systems led me to consider studying engineering, but lingering in the back of my mind were those deep thoughts of becoming a pilot. The thought of being in the cockpit, hands on the controls, maneuvering the plane where I wanted with the soothing hum of the engine in the background, was exhilarating. I imagined soaring above the family farm and fields where I had spent countless hours working, seeing it all from a bird's-eye perspective that was only seen in pictures. The vision was intoxicating, a calling that captivated me.

This final year of high school was a whirlwind of new-found freedom. With my driver's license, a steady job, money in my pocket, and my own truck, I felt a sense of independence I had never experienced before. Adding to the excitement, I found myself in a serious relationship with someone I'd met on the cross-country team. Dating was unfamiliar territory, as I had always focused on sports, school, and friends, never really making time for relationships. But now, I was navigating the excitement and complexities of having a girlfriend, adding yet another layer to an already-transformative year.

The year had all the ingredients for creating lasting memories, and I was absolutely soaking it all in—falling in love, excelling in school, and feeling like I had life all figured out. Not only did I have my last year of high school mapped out, but I had also planned the next decade: college, flight school, marriage, kids, and a family. Everything seemed to be falling into place perfectly. Heck, we even qualified for the cross-country state championship that year. I couldn't help but think, *What could possibly go wrong?*

Being accepted into the University of Wisconsin-Madison was a huge milestone, but receiving the Naval Reserve Officers Training Corps (NROTC) scholarship made it even sweeter. It was the beginning of the path toward both of my dreams: becoming a mechanical engineer and now having the opportunity to become a navy pilot. Everything seemed to align perfectly: college, a clear career path, and staying near my high school sweetheart and friends. I was living life in the moment, full of excitement for the future, with aspirations and dreams that stretched far beyond my small-town roots. I felt like I was on the verge of something big, something life-changing.

High school graduation was a thrilling moment. With just ninety-one students in the class of 1991, there wasn't a single person I didn't know on some level, making the experience feel all the more intimate. It wasn't just about walking across the stage to receive a diploma; it was the feeling of standing on the edge of the next chapter while being wrapped in the comfort of lifelong friendships. Our small, tight-knit class made the graduation celebrations feel endless, and I lost count of how many parties I attended. To celebrate my own achievements, I had three distinct parties. The first was an intimate family gathering; the second was a celebration at the Maple Tree restaurant, where I had worked since I was fifteen; and the grandest of them all was a party at the farm. My friend's band played in the shed, and it felt like the perfect representation of my life, bringing my high school friends together with my farm family and community, blending the two worlds that had shaped me. When the parties were over, marking the official end of high school, we never really said goodbye to each other; instead, we shared stories, laughter, and toasted to the best of times. We celebrated like nothing would ever change, even though, deep down, we all knew that it would.

CHAPTER II

The summer between high school and college felt like a dream, one of those rare golden moments in life where everything aligns so perfectly. The weight of high school lifted, replaced by a well-earned sense of accomplishment, and college was on the horizon, full of promise. I walked with confidence, pride, and maybe just a little too much optimism and arrogance, fueled by the fierce belief that I was destined to become a navy pilot. Looking back, I realize I probably leaned a little too hard into that mindset, but at the time, it felt like nothing could shake me. I don't remember a single bad day that summer.

All too quickly, the season slipped away, and before I knew it, the day had come to pack my truck with the college essentials. The boxes, bags, and stereo with select cassette tapes were now stacked neatly, ready for the journey. Though the thought of leaving was bittersweet, I found comfort in knowing I could always return on weekends to grab anything I had forgotten or just for a taste of home. My parents, as always, were there to lend a hand, carrying boxes up the stairs and helping me set everything up. Together, we had crafted a careful plan to avoid the hassle of a lengthy move-in, opting to take advantage of the stairs instead of waiting in the long line for the dorm elevators.

Once everything was in place, my new space felt both exciting and surreal. It was just a room, yet it was brimming with the possibility of new beginnings. I stood there for a moment, taking it all in, wondering just how many times I would fall out of that lofted bed this semester. After a quick goodbye to my parents, who I could see were both proud and a bit emotional, I wandered the dorm floor. Following the hum of chatter and laughter, I met future friends and savored the excitement of a new adventure that was about to unfold.

College proved to be more difficult than expected. The academics were demanding, and, for the first time, I had to learn how to study effectively. On top of that, the NROTC program compounded the layer of difficulty. Every Tuesday morning at five o'clock, we mustered for training, learning the fundamentals of military life. We prepared and wore our uniforms, drilled standard military terminology into our heads, and marched tirelessly around the indoor practice field of the Wisconsin Badgers football team. By the time I graduated, I was convinced that I had stepped on every square inch of that artificial turf.

Sports and athletics became a vital outlet for me during those years. I played club ice hockey, which kept me competitive and active, while also traveling to other NROTC units in the conference for sailing regattas and flag football tournaments. Those trips turned into some of the best times of my college experience. They weren't just about the competitions but were also about bonding with my fellow midshipmen, exploring new campuses, and embracing the camaraderie that came with being part of NROTC. Much like high school, where I'd balanced two separate lives between McFarland and the farm, it was very much the same with my dorm friends and my NROTC family. On one side, there were the casual hangouts and late-night talks with my roommates and dorm friends. On the other, there was the structured, disciplined world of NROTC, where bonds were forged through early mornings, demanding physical training, and shared purpose. Both worlds were distinct, yet they blended seamlessly, each offering its own sense of belonging and shaping me in different ways.

And, of course, I kept running. Even though I didn't have the speed to make the cross-country team at Wisconsin, running became my personal sanctuary. It was my time to process everything and clear my head of the challenges of academics, relationships, and anything else weighing on my mind. When I laced up my shoes and hit the pavement, it was like a reset button. Running gave me a sense of discipline and control in a world that was quickly becoming increasingly complex. It wasn't just physical; it was a mental and emotional release, a way to navigate the chaos with clarity.

The freedom of college life was exhilarating. Freshman year was all about meeting new people, forging lifelong friendships, and staying focused on academics to maintain a 3.0 GPA or higher for my NROTC scholarship to take effect sophomore year. Establishing a routine came easily, allowing me to balance school, a weekend job at the Maple Tree restaurant, and time with my girlfriend, who had two more years of high school.

In the midst of enjoying those first few months, I received a phone call from my dad. He informed me that he and Mom were getting divorced. While I appreciated the call, the real surprise came when he told me they were both moving into single apartments, leaving me without a home or bedroom. I was thankful for the chance to catch up with my dad, but I failed to realize that, come winter break, I would need to find a place to stay when the dorms closed for the holidays.

Despite having lived in Wisconsin my entire life, I was unprepared for the harsh reality of walking to class through snowdrifts, especially on Tuesdays when we were required to wear our designated navy uniform all day. As luck would have it, the heaviest snowstorms always seemed to hit on Monday nights, leaving me to trudge through deep snow from my dorm to the NROTC unit at 5:30 a.m.

My last final exam was scheduled just before Christmas Eve, and I was eager to finish the fall semester and spend time with extended family in celebration. With plenty of bedrooms for guests on the farm, I had a place to stay during the few weeks of winter break. Beyond that, and looking ahead to the summer, I knew I'd need to find a place to stay but presumed that I had plenty of time to figure it out.

Spring semester brought warmer temperatures—above freezing anyway—and I started to think ahead to the summer. With freshman year wrapping up, I began searching for a full-time summer job to complement my current part-time job. Eager for something different and fun, I landed a position at Skipper Buds, a local marina on Lake Mendota. My role focused on a mix of sales support, marina upkeep, and running the parts store, but I spent most of my time outdoors preparing boats for the showroom and test drives. There was always a demonstration boat in the water, and with convenient access to it after hours and on weekends, I couldn't resist the opportunity to get out on the lake.

With the University of Wisconsin-Madison nestled on the shores of Lake Mendota, it wasn't long before I started picking up college friends from the campus pier for weekends filled with water sports and lake adventures. The crisp, cool water became our playground, where we'd spend hours on the lake, meeting up with other boats or just drifting with the current. Already accustomed to driving our boat with my dad and sailing navy boats, learning to drive and navigate much larger powerboats felt like the perfect addition to my skill set as I looked ahead to a future in the navy.

With all the excitement of college, finding a place to live for the summer somehow slipped through the cracks. Since I didn't have much to move out of the dorm, I figured I'd just crash on my dad's couch until something more permanent came along. But with a full-time work schedule and the goal to save money for the next school year, a few days on the couch quickly turned into the entire summer. While I stayed there occasionally, I ended up spending most of my time with my girlfriend at her parents' house, a routine that carried over into the summer after my sophomore year as well.

I moved into an apartment for my junior year, finally free of the question of where I would stay during the summer. It was my first time living completely on my own, and while it felt like a big step toward independence, I couldn't help but miss those nights crashing at my dad's place. I missed the spontaneous adventures and the extraordinary conversations that, at the time, seemed like nothing more than casual chatter. We were so close that on weekends, if he'd had a tough week, he'd call me, and I'd invite him to whatever party I was at or hosting. Drinking with my dad in college was a blast. Sure, we received a few awkward looks from people who didn't know us, but it never mattered. We shared toasts, laughed, and just enjoyed those moments together.

Near the end of the fall semester, tragedy struck again. I was driving with a friend in my trusty, partially rusty Toyota truck to a neighboring town, where we planned to catch a basketball game on a cold December day. We were cruising down the highway, lost in casual conversation, when suddenly, a deafening *crack!* shattered the moment, followed by a relentless thumping against the back of the cab.

Alarmed, I eased the truck onto the shoulder, and we stepped out to investigate. Circling the truck, searching for visible damage, I expected to find a flat tire or fluid leaking, but everything looked surprisingly normal. I popped the hood, and still nothing. The engine ran fine. Just as I was about to climb back in, something caught my eye. The front of the bed topper was jammed up against the back of the cab, far closer than it should have been.

Stepping backward for a better view, a sinking realization set in. The entire frame was sagging in the middle. I crouched down to look underneath and found that it had rusted through and broken in half. The only two things holding it together were the drive shaft below and the bed topper pressed against the cab above. That rhythmic sound we had heard was the entire truck flexing, like a slinky toy, as we'd driven down the road.

Without cell phones in those days, our only option was to limp the truck to my dad's place, which luckily wasn't far. We crawled along at thirty-five mph, hazard lights flashing, listening to the unsettling sound of the topper crashing into the cab as we bounced down the highway.

Lost was my first love, a truck taken too soon by the unforgiving, salt-laden roads of Wisconsin winters. But with loss came opportunity. My uncle just happened to manage a car dealership in Madison, and I stopped by one day to say hello. During that visit, I happened to see a brand-new 1995 Nissan pickup in the lot with a low price that I just couldn't pass up. Maybe I'd learned something watching my dad haggle for hours when we'd purchased that first truck, or maybe I knew the manager, but either way, I drove home my second love that day.

In the fall of 1995, I entered my final year at the University of Wisconsin-Madison, eager for the challenges ahead. As an engineering mechanics major, I embraced the rigor of advanced coursework, while as a midshipman in NROTC, I counted down the months until graduation and my commissioning as an ensign in the US Navy. Just beyond that, I would begin Aviation Preflight Indoctrination in Pensacola, Florida, the first step in the demanding naval aviation training pipeline for aspiring navy pilots. I was exactly where I had always dreamed of being, living out my childhood dream and standing on the verge of flight school and the journey to becoming a navy pilot. With the finish line in sight, I savored every moment, lost in daydreams of the future that awaited me in the skies.

Midway through the fall semester, there was the perfect Friday afternoon, the kind of day that felt almost frozen in time. With temperatures dropping, the leaves had turned brilliant shades of red and gold, and the air was ideally crisp for another memorable afternoon run. My Walkman, loaded with my favorite Whitesnake cassette, was clipped firmly to my running shorts. I pressed play, placed the headphones over my backward baseball cap, and set out on my routine five-to-ten-mile run.

Wisconsin in the fall is breathtaking, a landscape painted in vibrant colors and dotted with rolling hills and sprawling farmland, the perfect backdrop for a long, unhurried run. I had no set route in mind, letting my legs and curiosity determine the path and distance. Everything about that day felt ordinary yet extraordinary, a fleeting moment of pure freedom. The steady rhythm of my footsteps and the music in my ears made the run a welcome escape from the pressures of school and life.

My final mile routinely led me through the engineering side of campus, a perfect cooldown and a chance to admire the campus architecture, creating a lasting memory. About a half mile or so from my apartment, a sudden, searing pain shot through my upper left shoulder blade, forcing me to gasp for air. Instinctively, my first thought was that I had been stabbed. I whipped my head around, searching for some unseen assailant, but no one was there.

Panic surged through me as the pain remained sharp and unrelenting, each breath a struggle. I slowed my pace to a leisurely walk, my mind racing through an amateur medical self-assessment, desperately trying to make sense of what was happening. Why was there so much pain in my left shoulder, and what could be the cause?

The pain gradually diminished slightly after some time back at my apartment, but an unsettling sensation lingered. Any sudden movement, such as jumping or stopping abruptly, triggered a strange gurgling sound in my upper left chest, reminiscent of water sloshing. The realization hit me in a second wave of panic. Something was seriously wrong. I fought to steady my breath as my mind struggled to make sense of what this could mean for my future as a navy pilot. The physical pain and the mental weight of uncertainty pressed down on me, and for the first time, I felt real fear that the dream I had worked so hard for might slip through my fingers.

The rest of the weekend followed a familiar and normal routine that was anything but normal. On Friday night, I met some friends for drinks at a smoky, crowded bar, casually sharing my story about the sharp shoulder pain during my run. We laughed it off, and the conversation drifted to other topics as the evening unfolded, much like any other outing. But when I lay down to sleep that night, the discomfort intensified. My left shoulder ached more than before, and my breathing rate was slightly elevated, just enough to make me aware. I tried to settle into sleep, but the nagging sensation would not let my mind rest.

By Saturday morning, I woke up feeling much better, convincing myself that whatever had happened wasn't significant. Pushing aside any lingering doubt, I packed my backpack and headed to the library, ready to lose myself in a few hours of studying.

Deeply immersed in studying, I barely noticed any lingering pain until I stood up to stretch my legs. As I wandered through the library, I noticed that my breathing rate was more rapid. The sharp pain had dulled, but an uneasy sensation remained. A wave of panic washed over me once more, prompting me to pack up my study materials and head back home to lie down and rest.

After a lengthy nap, I woke up feeling noticeably better and joined my roommates for dinner and drinks. The table was alive with conversation and laughter, but I felt distant and withdrawn. I sat there, participating in the chatter, but my mind was elsewhere, consumed by the rhythmic rise and fall of each breath, the unanswered questions gnawing at the edges of my thoughts. I smiled, laughed, and nodded as if I were present, almost on autopilot, but inside, there was a quiet yet intense deliberation of thoughts. I argued with myself but was still unable to determine what was happening and why.

By Sunday afternoon, I finally mustered the courage to visit the emergency room at the University of Wisconsin hospital. As I approached the front desk, my breathing was erratic, fast, and shallow, as if I had just finished a sprint. I did my best to recount my symptoms to the nurse, detailing the strange sounds emanating from the top of my left lung and the unnerving rapid breathing rate. Experiencing significant discomfort, the nurse handed me a clipboard and instructed me to take a seat and complete the required paperwork.

After what felt like an excruciating forty-five-minute wait, panting like an exhausted dog in the waiting room, I returned to the front desk and asked when I might be seen. The nurse asked me to continue waiting, so I handed her the clipboard with my paperwork and walked out of the emergency room in frustration. I drove myself home and immediately lay down, which was the only position that provided me with any relief in my given condition.

I woke up on Monday morning with intense chest pain, my breathing rate extremely rapid and shallow. Still reeling from the frustrating emergency room experience, I made my way to the campus medical clinic just up the street, knowing they would be open during the week.

The nurse at the clinic immediately recognized my distress and ushered me straight to radiology for an X-ray. Once the scans were complete, I was led into a small patient room, where I waited anxiously, each breath more strained than the last. Just as my thoughts began to spiral, the door suddenly burst open.

A large man rushed in, pushing a wheelchair, his face stricken with panic. Without hesitation, he grabbed my shirt with both hands and lifted me up effortlessly, placing me firmly in the wheelchair and muttering something about getting to the hospital immediately. He wheeled me through the clinic's narrow hallways, skillfully dodging obstacles in our path. In seconds, we reached the back of a waiting ambulance. The hospital was mere minutes from the clinic, yet the trip felt like it lasted an eternity. I was disoriented and struggling to process the chaos around me, my mind wavering between confusion and fear.

The ambulance arrived at the emergency room entrance of the University of Wisconsin hospital, and nurses swiftly transferred me onto a gurney, rushing me to the operating room. As the medical staff cut away my shirt, a nurse caught my attention and softly asked me to lie on my right side. She gently grasped my hands, pulled them toward her, and asked me to look into her eyes. In that moment, amid the confusion swirling in my mind and the chaos of the surrounding environment, I felt an unexpected sense of comfort as I looked into her eyes. Just then, I felt the doctor's fingers pressing against my left ribs, methodically searching for something. Out of the corner of my eye, I watched him raise a scalpel and, with precision, drive it between his two fingers directly into my ribcage. A sudden, deafening rush of air filled the operating room, and agonizing pain, unlike anything I had ever felt, engulfed me. The pain consumed me, and everything went dark.

When I woke from my painful fainting episode, I was lying on my back, shirtless, with a long tube protruding from my ribcage at the site where the doctor had made the incision. A sharp, localized pain radiated from the wound, but my breathing rate had stabilized, and the dull, persistent chest pain was gone. The tube led to a device hanging beside me, partially filled with water, emanating a sound somewhere between a vacuum and a fish tank. I would later learn that the device was, in simple terms, a vacuum system designed to remove air from my chest cavity, allowing my lungs to fully expand to their nominal size.

After settling into my hospital room with a tube protruding from my chest and draining into the vacuum tank hanging on the end of my bed, the doctor stopped by to visit and provide an update on my condition. He explained that I had experienced a spontaneous tension pneumothorax, or collapsed lung, a condition that often affects young, tall, thin, athletic males—traits that fit me perfectly. He went on to describe how, in such cases, a slight bump or protrusion on the lung rubs against the chest cavity wall during exercise, gradually wearing it down and creating a thin spot in the lung tissue. This spot eventually bursts under stress, causing pain and allowing air to leak from the affected lung into the chest cavity, which increases pressure on the outside of the lung. This pressure causes the lung to collapse, either partially or completely. In my case, my left lung had fully collapsed, and my right lung had partially collapsed, shifting my heart and trachea over to the right side of my body. He then showed me the X-ray they had taken in the clinic, in which my trachea appeared like an upside-down question mark and my heart was shifted a few inches toward my right side. This is the "tension" portion of the condition, where the heart is under pressure, pumping against the external force, and could cease pumping at any moment. The doctor then explained the upcoming surgery procedure to me, detailing how he would staple the hole closed and perform a procedure called a pleurodesis, which would chemically adhere my lung to the chest cavity wall. This would immobilize the lung and greatly reduce the risk of experiencing another pneumothorax.

While this situation was undeniably traumatic, my mind could not escape the consuming fear and thoughts of how this would negatively impact my acceptance into flight school. As a future pilot, I would be subjected to changing pressures in the aircraft, and I couldn't help but wonder how this condition might jeopardize my entrance medical examination. How could I possibly pass the exam with rows of staples in my left lung and my lung "sticky glued" to my chest cavity? The uncertainty weighed heavily on me, drowning out all other thoughts and leaving me trapped in a relentless cycle of doubt and anxiety.

After receiving the news, a few friends and family members came to visit. I tried to explain what had happened, but the conversation felt strained and awkward. They understood the gravity of the situation and were careful not to mention anything that might cause me to panic further about my future. I kindly asked some of my friends to inform my professors about my hospital situation, requesting they bring my textbooks and any assignments when they had the time. I also informed the NROTC unit of what had occurred, and they kindly told me to focus on getting well without a mention of consequences affecting my flight school selection. This response, though well-intentioned, only increased the anxiety I felt about the future.

While I was recovering from surgery in my hospital room, the doctor stopped by to provide an update. He explained that the surgery had gone well, and I would need to spend a few more days in the hospital with the chest tube in place while the lung healed. He also mentioned that he'd discovered some infection and inflammation on the outer wall of my lung, likely caused by bacteria and secondhand smoke I had inhaled while my lung was leaking air. Surprisingly, this inflammation had helped my lung adhere to the chest cavity wall, and he prescribed some antibiotics to address the infection. But later that night, something went terribly wrong.

I developed a severe fever that quickly spiked to a staggering 106 degrees, and the pain in my chest became unbearable. Fear gripped me as I lay there, convinced that I might not survive the night. Desperate and unsure what to do, I reached for the phone and called my high school sweetheart, my girlfriend now of five years, pleading with her to come stay with me during this frantic time, even though visiting hours had long passed. She lived just down the street from me, and I hoped that her presence would bring me some comfort amid this terrifying ordeal.

I was anxious about my future and alone in that dark, cold hospital room, desperately needing her by my side to help take my mind away from the dark thoughts that refused to subside. Excited to hear her voice on the phone, the conversation quickly turned tragic as she fumbled for excuses to avoid coming to see me. And then the heartbreaking truth emerged: She had already moved on from our relationship but hadn't found the courage to tell me. No goodbye. No conversation. No warning. Just . . . over.

Of all the things unraveling in my life at that moment, I had believed our relationship was the one thing I could count on: the one constant, the one person who would be there. But now, in an instant, even that was gone. I hung up the phone, feeling the complete abandonment of life and everything in it.

If I had to pinpoint the instant when my entire life came to a screeching halt, when everything I had worked for crashed down upon me, that would be it. I remained paralyzed in that moment, trapped in an eternity of shock and disbelief. What was supposed to have been the perfect run on a perfect day had shattered into disaster, all because of a slight bump on the top of my lung. It was a seemingly insignificant moment that had triggered a tragedy of staggering, unknown proportions.

I was just months away from college graduation, on the brink of taking the greatest, most rewarding step into my future, and I found myself clinging to life, literally. My thoughts were consumed by the severe pain, a burning fever, and a desperate fear that I might not survive the lonely night. The life I had known was slipping away, and with it, the dream I had fought so hard to achieve was fading faster than I could grasp.

Lost in a hollow, numb state, I barely noticed the sunrise filtering through the curtains. The weight of exhaustion and pain blurred the passage of time. By midmorning, an unexpected onset of chills overtook me, my vision tunneling into a gray blur. Then, just as suddenly, my fever broke, but the overwhelming pain remained, a relentless reminder of everything I had endured.

To help manage the pain during my remaining days in the hospital, the doctor prescribed an on-demand morphine IV drip. From what I can recall, the morphine eased the pain when I pressed the button, but it also distanced me from the harsh reality of the moment. One memory remains seared into my mind: My school backpack, once resting against the wall in my hospital room, seemingly crawled up the wall, moved around the room, and hung itself on a wall hook. It was clearly a morphine-induced hallucination, yet it left me questioning what really happened in those last two disorienting days in the hospital.

Filled with anxiety, I had no comprehensible logic of what the day would bring after leaving the hospital. I had missed nearly three weeks of classes, my high school sweetheart had abandoned me while I was on my deathbed, and I was left to face an uncertain future in the navy. The confident vision I'd once had for the next decade had crumbled, leaving me wondering what the next few hours would bring. Everything I had known, everything I had counted on, seemed either gone or on the brink of a disastrous outcome.

While the internal chest pain had subsided, the incision pain between my ribs remained so intense that coughing, sneezing, or laughing felt intolerable. I wasn't sure if I could walk, get around, or even manage on my own. As I prepared for my discharge, the attending nurse removed the adhesive bandage holding my chest tube in place and asked me to take a deep breath in and hold it, and as I did, she yanked that tube out of my chest cavity as if she were pull-starting a lawn mower. I shrieked in excruciating pain, and before I could even catch my breath, she had bandaged the incision. Though I was still trying to wrap my mind around what was happening, my stay was complete, and I was discharged from the hospital on Thanksgiving Day, 1995.

My dad was there to pick me up from the hospital around midmorning, with the plan to stop by my apartment so I could shower and change before we drove to the family farm for our annual Thanksgiving celebration. While I was in no mood for a celebration of any kind, the idea of being around family and friends felt comforting. That plan, however, quickly unraveled as we started driving. With every bump, turn, or movement of the car, waves of excruciating pain radiated from my left rib cage. The 1.6-mile journey from the hospital to my apartment felt like an eternity. I remember holding my breath as long as I could during the ride, desperately trying to expand my lungs in any attempt to ease the pain. Clearly, there was no way I could physically endure the hour-and-a-half drive to the farm. When we finally arrived at my apartment, I thanked my dad for the ride, told him I would see him soon, and slowly walked inside. Every movement, no matter how small, sent a jolt of unbearable pain through me.

The silence in the apartment was deafening. There wasn't a phone call or visit from a friend, and my roommates were away for the holiday weekend. I sat alone, imprisoned by my own thoughts, wondering what to be thankful for when every movement triggered a significant wave of pain. Showers were abandoned and meals ignored. I slithered between the bed and the reclining chair in my room, each movement a slow, careful effort. Each breath was deliberate and gentle. The radio provided me with my only comfort, and certain songs offered a temporary escape from my internal dark thoughts and unsettling reflections.

I felt lost and hopeless, trying to calculate how I could possibly manage to carry a backpack and walk to class on Monday morning when I could not stand up straight and struggled to walk to the bathroom. But more than anything, I found myself painstakingly analyzing every possible scenario in which I could still become a navy pilot. The internal battle between holding onto positivity and confronting reality was far more grueling than I had ever anticipated.

I'd once held a clear vision of my future. Until that single moment, during a run on an otherwise perfect day, life had been moving steadily along my aspirational journey. But now, sitting alone in my room, all I could see was darkness ahead. I knew that I had to rebuild and forge a new path, whatever that might look like, but I felt trapped, bound to this room, lost in the silence of my own existence and the weight of my heavy thoughts.

My roommates returned on Sunday, and life slowly rekindled before my eyes. The four empty days of solitude had felt like an endless blur, each moment stretching on as if time itself had stood still. But when the silence lifted, the emptiness gave way to movement, growth, and healing. After another week of rest and recovery, I returned to class, working to catch up on missed assignments and exams. Despite being absent for almost a third of my scheduled classes that semester and missing key lectures and classroom discussions, I managed to finish with a respectable GPA. Life was far from normal, but it was moving forward.

Winter break provided the ideal opportunity to rebuild both mentally and, more importantly, physically. While I was not back to running just yet, my mobility had improved, and I could manage daily tasks with ease. Things were finally looking up, yet a looming decision awaited me upon my return for my final semester of college: Was I still on track for flight school, and would Pensacola, Florida, be my next destination after graduation?

That final semester passed in a blur. I felt numb, trapped in an endless cycle of trying to justify what had happened, searching for a cause, an explanation, or anything that made sense. Every cough, twinge, or ache in my chest sent me spiraling, convinced that my lung had collapsed again, or worse, that the other lung had collapsed. These thoughts consumed me daily. Desperate for an escape from my thoughts, I threw myself into celebrating those final few months of college with my friends, embracing the most exhilarating and reckless time of my life.

On a seemingly ordinary day midway through the semester, I received the news that I had been waiting for, that I would report to Naval Aviation Schools Command in Pensacola, Florida, in late summer to continue on the flight school path. That was the best news I had received in a long time, a glimmer of hope after months of uncertainty. Yet beneath the excitement, fear lingered. I knew the first major hurdle would be the rigorous medical examination that every prospective aviation student would face. I was happy and cautiously optimistic, yet I was still fully aware that my journey could be over before it even truly began.

Graduation day arrived, and while it should have been a moment of celebration and an exciting milestone in my life, there was a quiet underlying feeling of sadness. The vision I'd once held for this day had vanished in that hospital room, replaced by a reality I'd never anticipated. Soon, I would have to say goodbye to the close friends who had been my lifeline, pulling me back into the light from the depths of darkness where I had spent so many days. A walk across the stage, a mispronunciation of my last name, a quick handshake, and just like that, I had officially graduated. After a few pictures with family and friends, I headed home to change out of the cap and gown and dress into my choker-style service dress white uniform for my commissioning ceremony into the United States Navy later that day.

The ceremony took place at the Wisconsin State Capitol building in an intimate and deeply gratifying ceremony with most of my family in attendance. While graduation had been just a brisk walk across the stage, this time, the six of us getting commissioned were the focal point of the ceremony. We all received awards, and the commanding officer spoke kind words about each of us. As the ceremony drew to a close, we raised our right hands and recited the oath of office in unison. Once complete, I was first in line to receive my first official salute, a naval tradition where a newly commissioned officer presents a silver dollar in return to the enlisted person who renders the salute. With only a limited number of enlisted personnel available, I walked toward the command master chief. With the largest smile, I returned his salute and handed him my silver dollar in a grateful handshake. That rewarding experience momentarily lifted my mind from the present and illuminated a glimpse of a promising path forward.

After the ceremony, a small reception gave me time to catch up with my family. As the night wore on, I hugged each of them goodbye before heading to the bars to meet up and celebrate a little more with my college friends. When I walked into the bar in my service dress white uniform, I felt every head turn and look in my direction. In an instant, more girls approached me than in all my years of college combined. With a few thumbs-up and high fives from my friends, I closed out my college career with a degree, a job, and a smile.

CHAPTER III

The close bond that my dad and I shared was challenged the day I left for flight school. He was visibly saddened, yet proud. We spoke very little, neither of us knowing quite what to say. I found it difficult to mention to him what I'd gone through in that hospital room and that I was uncertain about passing the aviation entrance medical examination. The thought of what might happen if I didn't pass was too overwhelming to even contemplate, and I couldn't bear to voice that fear to him. It was impossible to capture in a few words the years we had spent together, nor could I fully grasp how different life would be for both of us from this moment on. We said our goodbyes, and with one last look, I was on my way.

The drive from Madison, Wisconsin, to Pensacola, Florida, felt both empty and endless. Alone, my thoughts scattered in every direction, often drifting to memories stirred by the songs playing on the radio. Before my lung collapsed, I had never envisioned making this journey alone, uncertain of the future, filled with doubt, and questioning the path ahead. But here I was, in that very situation, facing that very uncertainty. With each mile, I felt more lost, searching for any sign or sense of direction, desperately trying to find something that might guide me through this unknown.

Flight school was a melting pot of people from all over the country, each bringing their own unique mix of intelligence and maturity. I kept a low profile, focusing on activities that would help me rebuild both mentally and physically, never mentioning a word about my medical disposition. Our daily routine was to muster each morning for attendance, then spend the rest of the day as we chose until we were assigned a class start date for Aviation Preflight Indoctrination. This academic course, notorious for challenging those less inclined to study, covered aircraft systems and the fundamentals of aviation. It was the gateway before we were assigned to a squadron to begin flying.

During this waiting period, I gradually eased back into running and discovered ultimate frisbee and triathlons, two sports that not only reignited my competitive spirit but also helped me rebuild my strength and endurance. That was the perfect opportunity to move on from the past and redefine who I was and where I wanted to go. I kept my focus firmly on the present, determined to simply get through each day. I adjusted my expectations, setting them much closer to the present, and resolved to ride the path I was on without overthinking what lay ahead. Each run would be better, and every day, I would strive to become a little stronger without the weight of distant expectations bearing down on me.

Before being assigned a class start date, every incoming flight school student must first undergo a medical examination administered by the Naval Aerospace Medical Institute (NAMI). Those who pass receive an "up-chit," a medical clearance permitting them to participate in aviation training and operations. Those who do not meet the medical standards receive what naval aviators commonly call the "NAMI whammy," signifying medical disqualification from flying. For them, the dream of aviation ends there, and the navy reassigns them to a career other than aviation.

Upon arriving in Pensacola, I resided in temporary housing and barely unpacked. I avoided settling into an apartment or signing a lease until I faced the dreaded NAMI whammy myself. It wasn't denial, just a realistic assessment of my chances. With rows of staples in my left lung and a large incision scar on my side that was still sensitive to touch and movement, I knew the practical chances of passing the medical examination were less than ideal.

The day of my examination arrived, and it proved to be a very thorough and exhausting ordeal, stretching on for most of the day. Working my way through the assigned checklist and procedures, I reached the final stop with the flight surgeon, a physician specializing in the medical care of aviators. As I sat on the exam table, the weight of the anxiety and stress I had carried since the day that dreaded scalpel had first pierced my ribcage consumed me. I was desperate to hear the result, yet I could not imagine what my next steps would be, no matter the outcome. I felt frozen, trapped in that moment, unable to move until I heard the result.

The flight surgeon gently tapped on the door and stepped into the room; his expression was unreadable. I handed him my medical folder with all the records and exam results from the day. Without uttering a word, he began flipping through the pages slowly, making notes on a separate pad as he went. He paused on the form that described my pneumothorax history and viewed the X-ray film. His eyes lingered on the details, noting the staples in my lung, and then he quietly asked what I had been doing to address this condition. I took a slow, deep, deliberate breath, forcing myself to remain calm, and explained my focus on physical activities to rebuild my strength and endurance and how my lung had felt very strong. The silence that followed was incapacitating. In those few seconds, every fear, doubt, and agonizing thought I'd ever had flashed through my mind. Then, breaking the silence, the flight surgeon said that everything looked good as he signed my up-chit and handed it to me. I sat in that moment for a few seconds longer, trying to comprehend what had just happened. Then, with all the strength I could muster, I clutched the up-chit with both hands and hurried to the parking lot, driving away as quickly as possible before he realized his mistake.

To say I was ecstatic would be an understatement. I had overcome what had once seemed like an insurmountable barrier. However, as the reality of the situation set in, I realized I had never truly envisioned or planned for what would come next. For so long, my sole focus had been on reaching this moment that I hadn't allowed myself to think or plan beyond it. The surge of excitement faded quickly, giving way to panic and the pressing need to find an apartment and unpack my belongings.

Since that pivotal moment in college, a quiet voice of doubt had lingered in my mind, a constant reminder of how quickly life can change. Now, standing at the threshold of this new chapter, I realized just how much my perspective had shifted. I no longer peered far into the future, meticulously planning a long and predictable course as I once had. Instead, I focused on the present, always calculating contingencies, bracing for the unexpected, and preparing for the next obstacle that might derail my intended path. It was exhausting.

With the up-chit in hand, I was assigned an Aviation Pre-flight Indoctrination start date, joining many of the remarkable people I had come to know over the past few months, forging lasting friendships. The course was both intensely competitive and academically demanding, requiring far more studying than I had ever managed in college. After a whirlwind of classes, exams, and a week in water survival training, I successfully completed the course and was assigned to the Red Knights (VT-3) squadron in nearby Milton, Florida, where I began training in the single-engine T-34C aircraft, marking the start of the next chapter in my aviation journey.

My first flight in the T-34C was everything I had imagined and more. From the moment I stepped onto the flight line, the symphony of sounds and the distinct scent of aviation jet fuel created an electrifying atmosphere and memory that will be forever entrenched in my mind. The experience began with a preflight brief, during which the instructor drilled me with questions to ensure I was prepared for the flight. Then, in the ready room, I donned my helmet and strapped on my vest, feeling the bulkiness and weight of all the survival gear firmly secured against my body, adding to the gravity of the moment. As I walked with my instructor across the flight line to our assigned aircraft, I deliberately slowed my pace, absorbing the lingering smell of jet fuel exhaust, the rhythmic hum of engines and propellers, and the sight of aircraft lined up in perfect rows, while others taxied to and from the runway.

It was the moment I had dreamed of for years, now coming to life in a way I would never forget.

The exhilaration of taking to the skies was undeniable, but I quickly learned that flying was much more than just the thrill of being in the air; it was an intricate and demanding skill. Staying ahead of the aircraft mentally was critical, a stark contrast to the carefree, scenic flying I had once envisioned. Every moment in the cockpit required precision, discipline, and relentless focus. The challenge wasn't just about flying but about executing and demonstrating knowledge of normal and emergency procedures flawlessly while keeping up with the instructor's ever-evolving training scenario and questions. It was easy for student pilots to become overwhelmed, and mistakes were an expected part of the learning process.

The flight school instructors were experienced pilots from every type of navy aircraft, offering an opportunity for us students to learn more about the navy through their diverse knowledge and perspectives. This was invaluable, as we often asked them about the pros and cons of their aircraft and overall experience, knowing that in just a few months, we would be submitting our individual "dream sheet," ranking the navy aircraft we desired to fly. Beyond their insight, these instructors also held the key to earning top grades on each flight, making it essential for us to show interest, even if their aircraft wasn't our top choice.

There were a few instances when we completed all the training objectives with a little time to spare. On one such occasion, we were cruising at around five thousand feet on a cloudy day. The kind of day where the clear blue sky was filled with giant cotton ball-like clouds. Still early in my training syllabus,

I was required to remain clear of the clouds, as I wasn't yet qualified to fly in instrument meteorological conditions, when pilots rely primarily on their flight instruments with limited to no visibility. But on this particular day, my instructor set the power lever and challenged me to navigate through the clouds up ahead without actually entering a cloud, effectively cloud surfing. I entered the first cloud tunnel and maneuvered the aircraft, weaving through the gaps, trying to stay clear while keeping my bearings. While that wasn't part of the official syllabus, it became one of the most invaluable lessons of flight school, forcing me to scan my instruments to ensure the aircraft remained safe while keeping my eyes and thoughts outside to stay ahead of the fast-moving, ever-changing sky.

The next phase of training took me to Corpus Christi, Texas, where I joined the Wise Owls (VT-31) squadron. The intensity of the program remained high, but now I was flying a larger, twin-engine aircraft, the T-44A. Unlike the single-engine trainer I had flown previously, on which the propeller was aligned with the fuselage, the T-44A featured engines mounted on the wings above each landing gear. This transition introduced a new level of complexity, particularly in mastering engine-out procedures and executing simulated single-engine landings. In this simulation, both engines operated normally, but we could only use one engine to land safely; the instructor held the other engine at idle but could add power if needed. I also had to contend with asymmetric thrust, which demanded heightened coordination, quicker decision-making, and a deeper understanding of aircraft dynamics.

I progressed through flight school without incident, and in February 1998, I earned the coveted title of naval aviator.

In a moment of immense pride during our winging ceremony, my parents pinned those pilot wings of gold onto my uniform, a moment I had dreamed of for years. This was heaven. This was exactly where I needed and wanted to be. I had passed the rigorous NAMI medical examination and defied the doubts that had once consumed me. I was finally on the verge of living my lifelong dream. In that moment, it all seemed so clear; the collapsed lung was nothing more than a small misfortune, just a minor detour on my journey. Right?

After the formal winging celebration with my flight school classmates, I relocated to Jacksonville, Florida, to join the Pro's Nest (VP-30) squadron, where I began training to fly the P-3C, the aircraft that would define my navy career. The pace was relentless, with a mix of classroom instruction, simulators, and training flights driving me forward. Now flying an aircraft with four engines and adding the complexity of both mission and weapon systems, there was far more to learn than simply how to fly an airplane. During classroom instruction, we traced hydraulic fluid through propeller and landing gear systems, memorizing the operation of every valve, component, and switch. We mapped electrons through nearly every wire on the aircraft, studying the power sources for each switch and relay, which would be critical knowledge in the event of an in-flight emergency. The depth of training was vast, but it was all part of preparing for the challenges ahead.

In my free time, I immersed myself in running and triathlons, pushing my body to redefine its limits. The intense training became my way of asserting control, a mental barrier I built to shield myself from the fear of another setback. I convinced myself that my past medical issues were firmly behind me, that

I had overcome them, and that nothing could stand in my way. Each day was meticulously planned around my triathlon training program, and each step was to prove to myself that I was stronger than the challenges I faced.

I carved out time to swim laps at the pool, refining my technique and searching for that perfect stroke, all while building endurance in preparation for racing longer triathlons. I also joined a local bike racing team, with whom I was able to significantly improve my cycling strength and endurance. Training became more than just physical preparation; it became a source of strength, both mentally and emotionally. It also provided an opportunity to meet and connect with new people outside of work to enhance my work-life balance.

As my time at VP-30 neared its end, my focus shifted to my first operational squadron assignment. This was a pivotal moment, filled with anticipation and excitement. Each of us students filled out our "dream sheet," ranking our preferred geographical locations from the four P-3C operating bases, hoping to be granted our top choice. The stakes were high; we all knew that not everyone would receive their top choice, as we would likely be evenly distributed among the locations. It was an exciting time, our first step into the operational navy, filled with the promise of new challenges and opportunities.

Yet, despite the excitement, an unshakable feeling of unease lingered beneath the surface. I couldn't quite place it, so I ignored it, choosing instead to push forward with unwavering determination. My lung had held up through flight school, through the rigors of training, and every physical challenge I'd thrown at it. There was no reason to doubt myself now. Or so I tried to convince myself.

I received my top choice to stay in Jacksonville and joined the Pelicans (VP-45) squadron, which was deployed to Puerto Rico. Once I received orders, the command reached out to coordinate the logistics of my arrival and to see how quickly I could join them on deployment in Puerto Rico after training was completed. It was a thrilling assignment, and I was excited to deploy and start flying operational missions overseas.

During my last few weeks of training in Jacksonville, I began to notice something unsettling. When lying on my right side, I felt pressure in the left side of my chest. Not a sharp or piercing pain like the past lung injury but a dull discomfort that made breathing feel labored. Sleep became difficult, and an unfamiliar sense of physical awkwardness settled in. With my next major career milestone right in front of me, I did what I had always done and chose to ignore it. I convinced myself that it was nothing, just a passing discomfort. And so, when the time came, I boarded the plane to Puerto Rico, determined to move forward, no matter what.

CHAPTER IV

In a warm and welcoming gesture, my fellow aviators greeted me with a cooler of beer as I stepped off the plane in Puerto Rico, instantly making me feel like part of the family. After settling into my room, I was up in the air the very next day, flying my standardization check ride, a quick familiarization flight during which new pilots are assessed and validated as proficient before flying with their assigned crew. I passed my check ride, and just a week after my arrival, our crew departed for Panama City, Panama.

We were flying missions nearly every day, and I was having the time of my life. Each crew contained eleven people and operated on a strict yet varied schedule, so we spent most of our days together and saw other crews every so often in passing. The camaraderie within a crew was an integral part of flying each mission. We continually joked, laughed, and shared countless moments, whether in the air or relaxing between flights, creating memories that would last a lifetime. This was everything I had dreamed of, and I could not imagine being anywhere else. I had moved on from the challenges of the past and had the entire world in front of me, full of endless possibilities.

I continued to ignore the troubling and abnormal physical symptoms that were affecting my daily life. What had started as dull chest pain and sleepless nights soon escalated with symptoms of severe itching. During flights, the bottoms of my feet would itch so intensely that I would remove my boot and sock, fiercely rubbing my itchy foot against the top of my other boot. The metal eyelets would scrape my skin raw and, in some cases, peel the skin from the underside of my foot. It was relentless, and no matter how much I tried to rationalize it, I couldn't ignore the fact that something was terribly wrong.

I didn't want to admit it. I feared that whatever this was might jeopardize my medical qualification to fly. The thought of this affecting my lungs, chest, or something even worse terrified me. I was slipping back into the same anxiety and dread that I had worked so hard to escape in the past. I felt trapped in a nightmare I couldn't outrun. The last thing I wanted was to face another setback in my career, but it felt as though the past was always lurking, threatening to pull me back.

Panama was a mix of new adventure and amazing delight, with misery sprinkled on top. The strange physical symptoms were worsening, and I wasn't sure how much longer I could hide them. After about a month in Panama, we returned to Puerto Rico for two weeks of training before a planned revisit. While back in Puerto Rico, I visited the squadron flight surgeon to discuss my new symptoms, including the small lump that had just appeared in the front of my neck. After examining me, he prescribed a round of antibiotics, suggesting that I schedule another appointment if the symptoms did not improve.

The symptoms improved slightly on antibiotics, so I chose not to revisit the flight surgeon, especially since we planned to return to Panama the next day. However, on the morning of our departure, everything changed. I woke suddenly and violently, sitting up in bed with a sharp pain in the left side of my back. The pain was so intense that I remained frozen in that sitting position, unable to move without worsening the pain. After an hour, the pain subsided just enough to allow me to slowly and carefully slither out of bed and get dressed. Every movement was deliberate and cautious as I tried to avoid aggravating the pain any further. With only a few hours before preflight began for our return trip to Panama, I visited the small medical clinic on base for a quick check-up, hoping to receive a bottle of Motrin or antibiotics to help provide some relief during the trip.

The doctor on call examined my chest and the lump at the base of my neck, then ordered a chest X-ray. It was April 19, 1999, a day I would never forget. I sat there, anxiously watching the clock, as time seemed to drag on endlessly. With preflight scheduled to begin in about thirty minutes, I couldn't shake the feeling that I was running out of time.

The X-rays were finally taken, and since it was the pre-digital era, I had to wait patiently in the examination room while the film developed. After what felt like an eternity—I was officially going to be late for preflight—the flight surgeon tapped on the door. He entered the room and calmly sat down across from me with a puzzled look. Without hesitation, he delivered the news: I would be medically evacuated (medevac) to the National Naval Medical Center in Bethesda, Maryland, the very next morning. The weight of those words hit me harder than I could have imagined, but I still couldn't fully process what he'd said or what was coming next.

I was furious, not just because I was going to be late for preflight but also because my trip to Panama had just vanished before my eyes. I had little to no concern for my health at the moment; all I wanted was to be back in the air, flying missions like I had dreamed about for so many years. The doctor provided little explanation, only mentioning that the trip was for some follow-up tests. I walked back to the hangar and informed my crew that I wouldn't be able to make this trip but would catch up with them in Panama in a few days. I returned to my room to pack for the morning flight, thinking it would just be a one-night stay in Bethesda. As I packed, I calculated my return, bringing along some study materials on the off chance I might be scheduled for a few pilot training flights later in the week before rejoining my crew.

I didn't sleep a wink that night. The excruciating chest pain and relentless itching left me feeling trapped in my own body. But even worse was the mental battle raging inside me. One moment, I reassured myself that this was just a minor setback and that I'd be back flying in no time. The next moment, fear paralyzed me, telling me that this was the end and that I'd be medically disqualified from flying. There was absolutely no one who could help to calm my thoughts or provide me comfort. I was completely alone in my own mind, forced to endure the gut-wrenching torment of these circular deliberations.

The next morning, the squadron flight surgeon accompanied me on the medevac flight to Bethesda. I was so consumed by anguish, doubt, and grief that I barely registered his presence and was in a confused mental state for the duration of the flight. My mind was a chaotic storm, unable to process anything beyond the fear gnawing at me. By the time we

CAPT Derek Adametz, USN (Ret.)

landed, I was sleep-deprived and mentally drained, stumbling into an unfamiliar reality. I couldn't remember the last time I had eaten, and I was completely unprepared for the jarring transition from squadron life to walking into a hospital, facing the unknown.

The flight surgeon guided me through a series of clinics for tests and evaluations. The initial examinations seemed routine—checking vitals, reviewing symptoms, and assessing the extent of whatever was wrong with me. We then reached a clinic that focused on the lump protruding from the base of my neck, and things took a more serious turn. The doctor suggested performing a fine needle aspiration to extract individual cells from the lump for further analysis. At that point, I was exhausted and just wanted it to be over, so I was up for whatever.

The doctor pulled out a device that resembled a medical syringe gun. A tiny needle affixed to a syringe protruded like a barrel from a device with a handle and a trigger. Without much explanation, I assumed the doctor would simply insert the needle into the lump and vacuum a few cells into the syringe. But after cleaning the area with antiseptic solution, he jammed the needle into the lump in my neck, withdrew it, then jammed it back in again, repeating the process over and over, like a boxer continually punching a heavy bag. The pain was intense, a sharp shock localized to my neck, but the surprise of the procedure left me almost numb to the physical sensation. This continued for what felt like an eternity, each jab adding to the discomfort. After what seemed like an endless barrage of needles, the doctor kindly said, "All done," as if I hadn't seen or felt anything and he wanted to provide me reassurance that the procedure was complete.

55

We then proceeded around the corner to a different room where another doctor would biopsy the lump, removing it from my neck to send to pathology. As I lay on the table in preparation for the procedure, the doctor peered at me with a puzzled look. He then mentioned that it would be too risky to numb the area because of where it was located on my neck. That didn't sound appealing, but again, I was so exhausted that I really didn't care.

He then placed a blue-and-white cloth over the area, carefully centering the hole in the middle over the lump. With most of my face covered, I couldn't quite see what was happening, only hear and feel. Just then, I heard the doctor say, "Here we go," and before I could brace myself, I felt the scalpel cut through my skin. The sharp, searing pain was unbearable. Every instinct screamed at me to pull away and run out of that room, but with the scalpel so close to my neck, I remained calm and still. He methodically sliced away a large portion of the lump, then continued cutting off layers for what felt like an endless amount of time. When he finally finished, he simply applied a few Steri-Strips to the incision and removed the cloth, and that was it.

He handed the container with the lump samples to the nurse, who promptly left the room, then explained that the lump was like a golf ball lodged behind my collarbone. Every time he sliced, more of it would pop out and reveal itself. He hadn't realized just how large it was and only removed a portion of it. So he left a half golf ball-sized lump floating around inside my neck. Thanks, doc! I thought the worst was behind me until the moment when the doctor asked me to proceed to the next clinic to provide a bone marrow sample.

Completely unprepared for this procedure, I had no idea what to expect. Sitting with me in the procedure room, along with my flight surgeon and a resident doctor, the surgeon calmly explained that he would be performing a bone marrow aspiration procedure, extracting samples from both sides of my hipbone. What he didn't mention was why they needed it or what exactly he was looking for, and by that point, I was too exhausted to ask and still reeling from the last two procedures.

As I lay face down on the exam table, the sting of the local anesthesia barely registered against the whirlwind of emotions swirling inside me. Out of pure reflex, I glanced over my left shoulder to see the doctor holding a razor blade in his hand and a large syringe with a hollow needle, about the size of my pinkie finger, resting ominously on the stainless-steel table beside him. In that instant, a wave of sheer panic engulfed me, but I forced myself to appear calm. Pressing my face into the pillow, I squeezed my eyes shut, desperately trying to shut out everything happening around me.

My first sensation was the pressure of the razor blade slicing through my skin, cutting down to the bone. A second later, an overwhelming force pressed into my hip. Telling myself not to look, I couldn't resist glancing over my left shoulder once more. I caught a glimpse of the doctor's feet leaving the floor as he leaned his entire body weight onto the needle, driving it firmly into my hipbone. Then, in an instant, a sharp *crack!* rang out, not just a sound but a shockwave that reverberated up my spine. The pain exploded through me, raw and unbearable. Before I could even think, a scream erupted from deep within me, louder than anything I had uttered before.

With the needle successfully pressed into my hipbone, every nerve in my body screamed as the doctor pulled back on the syringe plunger to extract the marrow fluid. There are no words to describe this kind of pain. My teeth sank into the pillow, my entire body locked—rigid and tense. When he finally removed the needle, I thought the torture was over.

Then, in a calm voice, he mentioned needing a bone sample.

Like he was hand drilling through a frozen Wisconsin lake with an auger for ice fishing, he inserted a specialized tool into the opening, twisting the handle as it scraped against my bone, carving out a fragment. Each turn of the handle sent fresh jolts of agony radiating through me, and I bit harder into the pillow, willing myself to endure this for just a few more seconds.

I had to remind myself to breathe, slowly allowing my body to unclench from its locked and rigid position. Relieved to have made it through a procedure of which nightmares are made, I barely had time to process the pain before the doctor reminded me that he needed to do the same on the other side.

Oh, holy hell!

As if doubling the agony was not enough, he handed the needle to the resident doctor, who would perform the same procedure on the other side under his supervision. My heart sank. I was certain that this second sample was less about medical necessity and more about giving the student some hands-on experience, at the expense of every nightmare I would have from now until eternity.

Luckily, or unluckily, that was the last procedure of the day, and we arrived at our final destination: the oncology clinic. I didn't even know what "oncology" meant when we walked through that door. As we sat in the waiting room, I glanced around and quickly realized that I was the youngest person by at least fifty years, which made me quite uneasy. On top of that, trying to sit comfortably with two freshly bandaged holes in my lower back was next to impossible.

Before long, we met with an oncology doctor who wasted no time delivering the news: I had stage IIA Hodgkin's lymphoma. I glanced around the room, unsure of who he was referring to, when I realized that it was me. First, I didn't know what "oncology" meant. Now, I had no idea what "Hodgkin's lymphoma" was. That was not my best day for a language exam.

I hadn't even checked into my hotel room yet when the oncology doctor informed me that chemotherapy would begin in just ten days, following a CT scan and a series of medical tests, including a gallium scan. Suddenly, I regretted packing only a single night's worth of clothes. He went on to explain that my treatment plan would consist of six cycles, encompassing twelve treatments, of ABVD (Adriamycin, Bleomycin, Vinblastine, and Dacarbazine) chemotherapy. The regimen required chemotherapy infusions every other Wednesday, with blood work on the Wednesdays in between. Adding to the surprises, the doctor mentioned a risk of sterility from chemotherapy and recommended that I visit the cryobank to preserve my sperm in case I wanted to have children in the future. He handed me a brochure for the nearest facility, and I stared at it for a moment. After an unusually long pause, the doctor's last words of the day were, "Congrats, this is like winning the lottery of cancers." The reality crashed over me with brutal force, leaving me reeling once again before I'd even unpacked.

On a somber day in April 1999, I walked slowly from the hospital to the bachelor quarters, just a short block away at the National Naval Medical Center in Bethesda, Maryland. After checking in and settling into my room for who knows how long, the flight surgeon departed shortly thereafter for the airport, heading back to Puerto Rico to rejoin the squadron. And just like that, I was alone, trapped once more in the suffocating silence of a darkened room, my life grinding to an unnerving halt.

I can't even recall my personal thoughts in the week leading up to chemotherapy and can only imagine that I was in complete denial, questioning everything I had ever known or done. Sleep remained elusive, the chest pain grew more unsettling, and the itching intensified, especially between my fingers and on my feet. My personal belongings remained in my apartment in Jacksonville, my deployment clothes and equipment were back in Puerto Rico, and I was stranded in Bethesda with nothing but a day's worth of clothing. I had no vehicle, no friends nearby, and no plan of what to do next.

I called my parents to tell them what the doctor had said. Within hours, they had booked the next available flight out of Wisconsin and would be here in a few days. They had jobs and responsibilities back home, so their visit would be brief. In the meantime, I would have to figure out a plan to survive in the bachelor quarters for the next six months.

Amid all the chaotic thoughts racing through my mind, one kept echoing louder than the rest: How could this all be happening again?

After a few days of drowning in self-loathing, I forced myself to rise from the misery and start over from ground zero once again. My first step forward was preparing for my parents' visit and my first chemotherapy session, which was now less than a week away. Life had to restart somewhere, so why not begin by pumping the most toxic chemicals imaginable into my veins, chemicals designed to destroy every rapidly reproducing cell in my body? Yeah, that sounded like the perfect plan.

There was a rental car agency on the hospital grounds, which struck me as surprising, though in hindsight, it probably shouldn't have. I rented a car, picked my parents up from the airport, and drove them to their hotel near the hospital. Despite having been divorced for a few years, they remained friendly and chose to share a room, which was a relief. It gave us a comforting place to sit, away from the sterile atmosphere of the hospital, where we could talk and try to find some semblance of normalcy in the chaos of the situation.

Spending time with them was calming, but they had many questions about the medical diagnosis and chemotherapy process, and I had no answers. I did my best to ease the uncertainty by sharing some details about my experiences in my first squadron, including my brief time in Panama. I described both the excitement of it all, along with the sleepless nights and the relentless itching that followed. It felt strange to talk about those days, as though they belonged to another life, distant and disconnected from what I was facing now.

We spent the next few days exploring the area together, doing what we could to make things feel as normal as possible. My parents helped me stock up on food and basic essentials for my room, offering a sense of comfort that I hadn't expected. Despite my mind constantly drifting toward the uncertainty of what my future would hold, having them there provided a small sense of reassurance and peace.

As their visit drew to a close, I suddenly realized that their departure coincided with my cryobank appointment. There wasn't enough time for me to return from the appointment to pick them up, and I didn't want to abandon them at the airport hours before their flight. After a moment of hesitation, I had no choice but to invite them along, planning to drop them off afterward. It wasn't ideal, but it was the only option I had.

We arrived at the cryobank facility, walked into an empty waiting room, and checked in with the front desk. Of all the things I could imagine doing with my parents, bringing them along to an appointment where I'd be providing a sperm sample for storage and preservation was at the absolute bottom of the list. After a brief wait, the doctor entered the waiting room and invited all three of us back to his office. I'm not easily embarrassed, but in that moment, the terror of humiliation and discomfort was knocking at the door. My mind raced, caught between fear of what was coming and the unsettling awareness that whatever he was about to say would change everything.

In his office, the doctor explained the entire procedure in a professional yet oddly parental tone, directing most of the conversation toward my parents as if preparing me for my first day of kindergarten. The next thirty minutes were a strange mix of awkwardness and enlightenment, an experience I hadn't quite prepared for. Afterward, he led us on a tour of the facility, walking us through the lab, which, to my relief, provided a temporary distraction from the uncomfortable reality of having my parents hear exactly what I was about to do next. Finally, he escorted them back to the waiting area while I was led to a small private room to complete the task, alone with my thoughts and the undeniable absurdity of the situation.

I took a few deep breaths, determined to focus and get this over with. After completing the task and sealing the sample container filled with what might just be my future children, I carried it to the lab, where the technicians eyed me like hungry wolves, eager to collect and process my sample for cryogenic storage. Their enthusiasm was unsettling, and I wasn't about to stick around for small talk. Wasting no time, I left the lab and turned down the long hallway toward the waiting area, expecting to find my parents in the same empty waiting room that we had left not long ago.

But when I walked through the door, I froze. The once-empty waiting room was now packed. I was already embarrassed about where I was, what I just did, and having to bring my parents along to experience all of this with me. Scanning the crowd, I spotted my dad in the back corner. Just as I started toward him, my mom looked up from her magazine, saw me, and, in a loud voice, exclaimed, "Wow, that was fast!"

I have never felt more embarrassed in my entire life.

Without hesitation, my dad wrapped an arm around my mom, pulled her from the chair, and whisked us out of there before I could hear a single giggle from the crowd.

The drive to the airport was mostly quiet, though my dad seemed to snicker under his breath the entire time. I dropped them off, we said our goodbyes, and they wished me luck with chemotherapy. "Luck" and "chemotherapy" were two words that didn't seem like they belonged in the same sentence, but I knew what they meant. Afterward, I drove back to the hospital grounds, returned the rental car, and slowly walked back to my room. Alone once again, I sat motionless, staring at the walls in complete silence, trying to imagine what chemotherapy would be like tomorrow.

My first walk into the chemotherapy room was haunting. The smell hit me like a ton of bricks, indescribable yet unforgettable. Then came the depressing sight of the oversized light blue vinyl chairs lined up against the walls, each paired with an IV pole—a stark, inescapable reminder of what awaited.

A nurse welcomed me and said that I could sit wherever I liked. She was kind and cheerful, almost too cheerful for a place so heavy with unspoken dread. A few other patients were scattered throughout the room, each lost in their own battles. I chose a chair away from the others, wanting nothing more than to disappear into the moment and get through this treatment.

The Wednesday of my first chemotherapy treatment became my first true lesson in expectation management. I had envisioned the nurse administering four quick shots, one for each of the ABVD chemotherapy regimens, much like receiving immunizations at a medical clinic. That illusion was far from reality.

The first hour was spent just inserting the IV into my arm and flushing my system with an entire bag of saline solution. Then came the chilling part. The nurse placed three large syringes filled with chemotherapy on the side table next to my chair. One fluid was bright red, one was yellowish, and the last was clear. The nurse detached the saline tube, sat down in front of me, and very slowly pushed the contents of each syringe directly into my IV over the course of two agonizing hours. Yep, two hours. I had already peed twice, and adding more fluid to my system wasn't helping the situation.

As soon as the first chemotherapy drug entered the IV, a strong metallic taste flooded the back of my mouth. The nurse reassured me that this was common and handed me a Jolly Rancher candy to help alleviate the taste. A bowl of Jolly Rancher hard candies always sat in the chemotherapy room, free for patients to grab before treatment. I've never been a fan of hard candy, but I was even less a fan of the metallic, penny-like taste of chemotherapy, so Jolly Ranchers it was.

Because the chemicals were so toxic, the process was painstakingly slow. The nurse would push a small amount, about two cc, directly into my IV, then pull back on the syringe plunger to ensure blood flowed back into the IV line before repeating the process. The nurse explained that the chemo was so potent that she must confirm the fluid remained in the vein, for if it leaked out, it would cause severe tissue damage. The thought of the chemotherapy drugs being powerful enough to dissolve the tissue in my arm was deeply unsettling.

After the nurse administered the three-syringe chemo-therapy cocktail, she brought over a small IV bag, about six inches by six inches and wrapped in a dark plastic cover, and hung it on the IV stand alongside a fresh saline solution bag. The nurse reattached the saline solution tubing to my IV and carefully adjusted the thumbwheel to regulate the amount of the final chemotherapy liquid mixed with the saline solution. Curious, I asked about the dark plastic cover. The nurse casu-ally explained that if exposed to light, the chemotherapy would degrade or even eat through the small bag. Nice. And this chemical was going into my body. I was at a complete loss for words at that moment.

No sooner had the nurse answered my question than I felt an extreme burning sensation coursing up my arm, like fire ants marching in line beneath my skin. Instinctively, I gripped my armpit with my other hand, squeezing as hard as I could to numb the pain in my arm, while the nurse adjusted the thumb-wheel to lessen the flow. The burning sensation eased from excruciating to merely agonizing, but now, with reduced flow, the already-grueling process would take even longer. For the next two hours, I sat there, watching the slow drip of clear fluid from the chemo bag, each drop a reminder of the poison burning through my body. Five hours after first settling into that chair, enduring what was undoubtedly the most miserable experience of my life, I completed the first of twelve chemo-therapy treatments.

As I left the clinic, I stopped by the pharmacy window to pick up a brown paper bag filled with pills, vials, and syringe needles. The pills were meant to combat the inevitable nausea that would soon take hold, while the vials contained Neupo-gen, a medication I would have to inject into my leg daily to stimulate the production of white blood cells to help fight off infections as chemotherapy slowly stripped away my immu-nity. The walk back to my room, though just a short block, felt like an eternity. The weight of the brown paper bag in my hand was nothing compared to the crushing weight of my thoughts. Each step felt heavier, and I struggled to process what had really happened, caught between disbelief and the sobering realization that this was only the beginning.

I woke the next morning to find that nothing had changed after treatment. My only solace was the familiar ritual of press-ing "play" on the Discman compact disc (CD) player I had brought with me from Puerto Rico. The comforting sound of Third Eye Blind's self-titled album, the only CD I had with me, filled my ears. Ironically, the very first track was *Losing a Whole*

Year, a cruel yet fitting title considering what lay ahead. Every morning began the exact same way, pressing play as I made my way to the bathroom. That album became my anchor, its songs forever embedded in my mind. A complete album in which every track felt eerily relevant to my situation and the struggles I was about to face.

I was alone in a vast city, grappling with the reality of what to do on the first day of the rest of my life. My first task was simple in theory: take the Metro to find where I could buy clothes and pick up a few basic necessities, anticipating that I would run out of what I had purchased with my parents. But in reality, the relentless chest pain, itching, and upset stomach from my first chemotherapy treatment turned even a simple errand into an exhausting ordeal. More than the need for supplies, venturing out into Washington, DC, helped me reclaim a sense of normalcy that I so desperately needed. It was a brief escape from the confines of the hospital grounds, with a chance to feel like a person again rather than a sick patient. However, during this reprieve, I learned my second lesson in expectation management. While I had accounted for carrying what I could manage, I neglected to consider the need to use both hands to itch between my fingers every few seconds. Frustration quickly replaced excitement, and before long, I abandoned my plans, returning to the hospital grounds with just enough supplies to get me through a week or so.

The next day, I reported to nuclear medicine for my gallium scan. On that day, the radiologist injected gallium, which is a radioactive material that binds to blood proteins, circulates through the body, and accumulates where there is inflammation or a tumor, into my vein. The following day, I returned to the clinic, where

I was instructed to don a hospital gown and lie on a cold, hard table, similar to an X-ray table. My feet and legs were gently taped together, and I was strapped down to the table to ensure I remained as still as possible, which on any other given day might seem disturbing. A large receiver box was then lowered over my entire body, designed to collect the radiation emitted from within me. This device would detect my Hodgkin's lymphoma by revealing areas of increased density around the tumors compared to the surrounding healthy tissue and provide more detail about the number of tumors and areas within the body that were infected.

Lying squished between the hard, cold table and the receiver box, I could just see the screen that displayed what the receiver was collecting. What began as a dark, empty screen soon morphed into a haunting image, like a skeleton emerging from a shadowy hallway. Before long, small white dots appeared along the outline of my body, and minute by minute, the density of those dots increased until my entire body was visible. My outline glowed in a ghostly way, but my chest was a disturbing contrast, scattered with numerous dark circular areas and a large prominent shadow on the left side. This stark and unsettling image served as a lingering reminder of the undeniable reality of what was unfolding within me.

When the scan was complete, the receiver box lifted, and I was finally freed from the confines of the table. After changing back into my clothes, I met with the radiologist one last time for some post-procedure instructions. He informed me that I would likely repeat the process after my fourth cycle, and the radioactive material would gradually decrease over the next few days through my urine and stool. Therefore, it was crucial to clean up any urine splashes, flush the toilet twice, and wash my hands thoroughly. I didn't know whether to laugh or feel concerned, my mind racing with the absurdity of it all. On the walk back to my room, I couldn't help but imagine making a T-shirt that read "Beware, Toxic Urinator on the Loose." It was a bizarre twist in an already-surreal situation.

Days passed in a blur, with no actual obligation forcing me out of bed each morning, except for Wednesdays. Nights offered little relief, as relentless itching and chest pain robbed me of any proper sleep. Though nausea had not yet set in, I still felt far from well. The long, solitary hours in my room encouraged me to seek any form of distraction. With cell phones becoming more available in 1999, I ventured out once more, hoping to purchase a phone and reclaim some connection with friends, family, and the world beyond the hospital.

The next Wednesday arrived, bringing about the routine visit to the oncology clinic for blood work. While there, the front desk scheduled an appointment with my doctor to review the blood work results, adjust my chemotherapy regimen if needed, and develop a schedule for routine CT scans and pulmonary function tests. The CT scans would be the primary way to see the reduction and elimination of tumors within my chest, and the pulmonary function tests would document any reduction in my lung capacity and efficiency, as the Bleomycin chemotherapy had the potential for life-threatening lung injury. What had once felt overwhelming was quickly becoming my new normal, a life structured around chemotherapy treatments and medical appointments and procedures. Not really the new start I was looking for.

My appointment with my oncologist finally arrived. Aside from our brief, somewhat awkward interaction after my long flight from Puerto Rico, this felt like our first genuine meeting. He was kind, polite, and informative, putting me at ease as we reviewed my blood work results. Considering I had only undergone one chemotherapy treatment, my results were fairly normal. Then, we turned to my initial CT, pulmonary function test, and gallium scan, which revealed a countless number of lymph node tumors in my chest and neck area and a large mediastinal mass in the center of my chest, which was likely the culprit behind the chest pain and labored breathing I'd experienced back in Jacksonville before deployment. The mass was the size of a baseball.

The doctor explained that he would closely monitor my upcoming scans, watching for the mass to shrink. He outlined the treatment plan, emphasizing that when the mass had become nothing more than a sliver of scar tissue with no discernible reduction in size from the last CT scan, I would undergo one final cycle of chemotherapy, which was expected to be the sixth and final cycle. Amid this dark discussion, I found a glimmer of hope, an end in sight after six cycles, if only my body could hold up long enough.

They say the anticipation of death is worse than death itself. That's exactly what Tuesday nights felt like, the restless, anxiety-filled hours leading up to my Wednesday chemotherapy treatment. If there was a means to escape the prison of my thoughts, I never found it. Each Tuesday night became a test of endurance, perseverance, and strength, while each Wednesday morning walk to the oncology clinic was an act of defiance, a commitment to fighting something aggressive and relentless that I could not see but sure could feel.

By the time I set foot in the chemotherapy room for my second treatment, I was already exhausted. This time, at least, I knew what to expect: the long hours, the slow drip into my IV, and the inevitable burning that would come at the end. The Jolly Ranchers added a nice touch, as I hardly recognized the metallic taste in the back of my mouth this time around.

In the days leading up to my second Wednesday of blood work, I purchased a cell phone. Now, back in 1999, it was just a phone, but it gave me a much-needed lifeline to stay connected with family and friends. While I expected this to be a welcome development, I quickly realized that conversations were difficult. Explaining my situation over and over was exhausting, and I could hear the hesitation as my friends often struggled to find the right words in response.

I also reached out to my squadron in Puerto Rico to provide an update. Since I was still officially attached to them, they continued covering the cost of my room, just as they would have if I were still deployed to Puerto Rico or Panama. On a whim, I asked if they could provide me with a rental car so that I could leave the hospital grounds to purchase necessities and find a small escape from the confines of treatment. To my surprise, they agreed. That day, with keys in hand, I found myself behind the wheel of a rental car, suddenly free to explore beyond the hospital walls and beyond the Metro stop locations, even if only for a little while.

The Wednesday of my third treatment had arrived, and I found myself once again in one of those beautiful light blue chairs in the chemotherapy room, receiving the initial saline solution before treatment began. By now, a disturbing pattern had emerged. A few days after each treatment, the vein used for the IV would harden, stiff like a pencil beneath my skin, only to fade away completely after another day or two. With two veins in my left arm already gone, I counted the remaining visible veins, wondering if I could, in fact, make it through all twelve treatments.

The nurse approached with the familiar three-syringe cocktail, sat in front of me, and began administering the chemotherapy into my right arm this time since the two best veins in my left arm were now disintegrated. As the nurse began pushing the contents of the second syringe into the IV, my right forearm became irritated. Severe itching was nothing new, and I had grown accustomed to it, but it usually occurred in familiar spots like my fingers and feet, occasionally elsewhere. Instinctively, I scratched my forearm, and almost immediately, it began to swell. That wasn't good. The nurse became concerned and immediately stopped administering the chemotherapy.

I watched helplessly as my arm swelled further while the nurses huddled together for a quiet discussion. Moments later, a nurse stepped forward and injected a small syringe of clear fluid into my IV, something to reduce the swelling so the treatment could continue.

What followed felt like the longest two hours of my life. I stared at the clock, watching that red second hand laugh at me with each completed rotation around the dial. Just when I thought I would never leave this chair again, the swelling dissipated, and the nurse resumed administering the second syringe. The pain and misery of treatment were just as relentless as before, but now with the addition of a long, agonizing two-hour intermission. Nine more treatments to go. Surely, it couldn't get much worse than that.

Another CT scan, more chemotherapy treatment, and more blood work, and I was two months into treatment with four more to go. A few observations to highlight now that I was a third of the way through: The relentless itching and chest pain had lessened, becoming far more tolerable. I had developed a heightened sense of smell, and not in a pleasant way. The scent of the hospital, especially by the galley, became deep-rooted in my mind, a permanent reminder of chemo's misery. My urine had taken on a vivid orange color thanks to the dark red hue of the Adriamycin coursing through my veins. My hair was noticeably thinning, though I hadn't quite reached the full "chemo patient" look. And the nausea intensified, particularly on the day after treatment, forcing me to begin taking the medication to lessen the impact.

Under the worst circumstances imaginable, I struggled to maintain a positive outlook while my body deteriorated before my eyes. The dream of returning to the air as a navy pilot, once my guiding light, was now overshadowed by doubt and uncertainty, not only about flying again but also about finding my way out of cancer itself. My routine had become familiar, comforting through predictability yet distressing with anguish and pain. Deep down, I sensed that something wasn't right. A quiet unease settled in, a nagging feeling that the road ahead held even greater challenges. I remained cautious of what awaited me on this difficult and unforgiving journey.

During the third month of treatment, around mid-June, I received Permanent Change of Station (PCS) orders in the mail, directing me to detach from the squadron and report to the Naval Historical Center at the Washington Navy Yard in Washington, DC, in July. PCS orders meant that, somehow, I had to figure out how to move all my belongings from my apartment in Jacksonville and find a new place to live in DC. Starting in July, the squadron would no longer be covering the cost of my room or rental car. I would have to fly to Jacksonville, pack up everything I own—except for my belongings still in Puerto Rico—retrieve my truck from long-term storage, then drive myself to DC. Yeah, no problem.

The most troubling part of this new circumstance wasn't the logistics of the move but receiving my orders in a stamped envelope addressed to a personal mailbox I had at the hospital without a phone call or prior notice. I understood the need to bring in a replacement pilot to fill the billet I was occupying, but after everything that I had endured, the silence hurt more than I could express. A simple phone call would have meant so much, a gesture to remind me that I wasn't entirely alone on this journey. More than that, it would have allowed me more time to prepare, both mentally and physically, for the immense challenges of moving in my current condition. The real sting, though, came from the sense of abandonment by the squadron that had once felt like family.

After discussing the situation with my doctor, I received the green light for the trip. I found an apartment in DC, returned the rental car, and booked a flight for the first week of July. I departed the Friday following my fifth chemotherapy treatment. Unfortunately, my nausea had worsened, and the medication had lost its effectiveness, making the flight incredibly difficult. Upon my arrival, a duty officer, who managed a small detachment in Jacksonville while the squadron was deployed, picked me up from the airport and drove me to long-term parking on base, where I retrieved my truck.

The effects of chemotherapy were beginning to take an assault on my body and mind. As I sat in that lot full of vehicles parked neatly in rows, each covered in a thick layer of dust from months of abandonment while their respective owners were deployed to locations around the world, I felt the full weight of isolation. The stillness of the scene around me only amplified the desolation I carried within.

For a moment, I simply sat there, staring at my truck, searching for any small sign of positivity in the day. With a deep breath, I turned the key in the ignition. The engine roared to life on the first crank after sitting idle for five months. A brief smile flickered across my face, perhaps the only one that day.

Wasting no time, I drove straight to my apartment to meet with the manager and terminate my lease immediately under military orders. With little expectation of returning to Jacksonville anytime soon, especially with my career as a navy pilot hanging by the thinnest of threads, I packed everything I could fit in the truck and discarded the rest. Though I had little physical strength or energy, I somehow managed to finish the task and hit the road.

The trip from Jacksonville to Bethesda was manageable, though the nausea was becoming a growing issue, forcing me to pull over several times along the way. By the time I finally arrived, exhaustion had set in. Still, I unpacked my things and did my best to make my empty apartment feel like home, even though it would only be for about four months.

I reported to the Naval Historical Center and explained my situation to the boss, who was incredibly understanding and accommodating, allowing me to attend to my medical appointments as needed. Having my own truck for transportation provided me a familiar sense of freedom, and work offered a much-needed stimulus, even on the toughest days. I hadn't fully grasped how unhealthy the isolation had been until I finally had a reason to leave my room and engage with the world again.

While I was excited to have a cell phone now, it remained mostly quiet. My friends and family were always happy to chat when I called them, but I rarely received calls. And whenever we spoke, there remained an unmistakable hesitation in their voices, a delicate balance between what to say and, more often, what not to say. I could sense their uncertainty, the way they tiptoed around certain topics, afraid of saying something that might remind me of my own mortality or stir up emotions during an already-difficult experience. The close friends I had once known so well in high school now became distant, as if my cancer had created an invisible barrier between us. It wasn't intentional, but my diagnosis made even simple conversations awkward. The calls and messages dwindled, and before I fully realized it, my relationships with close high school friends had all but become nonexistent.

Then one day, my phone rang. It was a great friend from flight school, calling as he drove from Jacksonville, Florida, to Brunswick, Maine, to report to his first operational squadron. He wanted to meet up at Camden Yards in Baltimore for an Orioles game. The invitation was unexpected, and for the first time in a while, I felt a genuine spark of excitement. I was thrilled at the chance to see him and escape, even if just for a few hours, into the real world. But as much as I looked forward to it, I couldn't help but wonder how I would feel or if my nausea would allow me to enjoy the company or the game. I wanted so badly for the day to feel normal, but deep down, I knew that nothing in my life felt normal anymore.

We met up, and from the very first moment, it was all smiles and effortless conversation. After all my worrying about whether things would be different, he just saw me and talked with me the same way he always had. He didn't look at me and see a cancer patient, underweight and losing my hair. He saw me, just as I was before cancer, and treated me no differently.

That day was exactly what I needed—to laugh, to joke, to break free from the prison of my own thoughts, and, for the first time in a long time, to feel like myself again. That simple interaction became the turning point in my treatment. It gave me the strength to keep fighting and became the moment I stopped seeing myself as a victim and instead found confidence to truly believe I could beat cancer. I owe so much to my friend and that one spontaneous phone call because, in the end, it wasn't about a baseball game. It was a reminder of who I was and who I still could be.

The start of my fourth cycle marked a metaphorical hump day in my chemotherapy journey. I was far from feeling well, but I also wasn't feeling as terrible as I expected, at least not yet. The worst of chemotherapy's side effects were knocking at my door, and I was turning the knob, only I didn't realize it in that moment.

I had settled into a routine of driving to work at the Naval Historical Center each day except Wednesdays. Being back in the professional environment, I formed real connections with my coworkers, engaging in meaningful conversations that gave me a sense of normalcy that I hadn't anticipated. Initially, the idea of working during chemo was distressing. But as the weeks passed, I found it was exactly what I needed, and it became a welcome escape from the isolation of my apartment and the ever-present thoughts of chemotherapy.

During my seventh treatment, an older gentleman walked into the chemotherapy room and sat directly across from me. I'd seen him around previously but never paid much attention. While it wasn't unusual for people to sit next to or across from each other, I had just always instinctively chosen a chair that was far from others. I preferred the distance, not wanting to engage with anyone in that sterile, dreadful place. As a result, I had never really spoken to anyone during treatment, aside from the nurses who came and went. The room, with its quiet hum of machines and heavy air of illness, didn't really invite casual conversations. It was a place and a time to get through, most people hoping to erase it from memory and not make any connections.

On this particular day, the older gentleman made eye contact with me and, in a quiet tone, asked what I was in for. I wasn't exactly well-versed in the proper etiquette of the treatment room, so I was caught off guard for a second. After a moment of confusion, I hesitantly shared that I had Hodgkin's lymphoma, then politely asked him the same question, unsure what to expect. He responded with a complex medical term that I couldn't quite grasp but then added nonchalantly that all the bone marrow in his body was dead. The starkness of his words hit me in a way I hadn't expected. His response was so raw and delivered with a quiet matter-of-factness that it nearly knocked me out of my chair.

When this gentleman sat in the chair across from me, his skin was ghostly, the color of a sheet of paper, and the dark liver spots scattered across his arms were more pronounced by the stark pallor of his complexion. After our initial introduction and exchange of our respective illnesses, we continued to talk, during which a nurse hung a bag of blood on his stand and connected it to his IV. Over the course of our conversation, the bag emptied, and his skin turned from pale white to light pink. After the nurse hung another bag, he continued to pinken up even further and now had a normal color and appearance.

While his treatment and condition were absolutely fascinating to me, they were nothing compared to the strength of his character. Our conversation was mostly small talk, but he offered to share more about his condition than I was ready to share about mine. He casually mentioned that he would visit the chemotherapy room every Wednesday, receive two bags of blood, then go about his life. His story captivated me, giving me a sense of hope and optimism that I hadn't felt in a while.

Suddenly, without really thinking, I blurted out a question that might have been a bit insensitive given the context, but I wanted to know more. I asked him why he would go to such lengths for treatment. He paused for a moment. His eyes welled up, and he said, "For my grandkids."

His response tugged pretty hard at the heartstrings, and I was without a word in response.

We talked a little while longer until his treatment was finished, then we said our goodbyes. As he walked out of the room, I sat in quiet thought, reflecting on my own journey, wondering what sacrifices I might have to make in the future to get through this.

Two weeks later, I was looking forward to seeing him again, even if it was just to say hello. But from that moment on, he never returned. I never saw him again, yet his story resonated with me then and still resonates with me today. A quiet reminder of resilience, love, and the reasons why all of us in that room continued to fight.

As I approached my fifth cycle, my confidence grew with encouraging results from my second gallium scan, but the physical toll from chemotherapy had worsened, and the side effects had intensified. My hair was falling out rapidly, and each morning I woke to find a dense halo of hair on my pillow. Rather than cling to what little hair remained, I shaved my head and embraced the bald look. It might not have been so bad if my eyebrows had stayed intact, but they fell out too. Now, I looked downright ridiculous.

The physical effects of Adriamycin were impossible to ignore. The deep red hue not only turned my urine a vivid orange but also left my skin with an unnatural matching tint. But the most brutal side effect was the nausea. What had once been manageable in earlier cycles had now become a constant and unrelenting presence. It became so severe that my body began reacting before chemo even started. The moment the saline solution was connected to my IV, I would start vomiting, a conditioned response, as if my body already knew the dread that was coming.

This continued throughout the entire treatment. At this point, I now needed two nurses: one to administer the chemotherapy and another to swap out my ever-present "puke bucket," as they called it. Nausea had become an inevitable part of each treatment, dragging out the process and causing frustrating delays. What used to be a five-hour session was now creeping toward eight hours.

In the beginning, the Jolly Rancher hard candies had been a brilliant idea to alleviate the metallic taste of chemo. I made a habit of grabbing a few on my way into the chemotherapy room to help me through each treatment, letting the sweetness dull the chemical bitterness that clung to my tongue. But not anymore. The first time I vomited with nothing but the overwhelming taste of artificial fruit in my mouth, something changed. From that moment on, the mere thought of a Jolly Rancher was enough to make my stomach churn. Even now, years later, that simple candy remains a visceral reminder of those endless hours sitting in that chair, staring into that bucket.

I was rapidly deteriorating from the effects of chemotherapy, unsure if I could continue this journey alone. Each treatment drained more of my strength, and I found myself nearing a breaking point, doubting whether I could endure another round. Just as I felt I was slipping beyond my limits, fate suddenly intervened in the most unexpected way.

A friend from Jacksonville, who was visiting her parents in Maryland, invited me to dinner with them. At first, it seemed like a simple gesture of kindness, but to my fortune, both of her parents were doctors. After all the chaos, isolation, and grief I had endured, this unexpected invitation felt like more than a meal—it was a lifeline, a much-needed opportunity to discover a renewed sense of hope.

A home-cooked meal was more delicious than words could describe, especially after months of hospital galley food and the occasional fast food indulgence. Her parents were incredible, kind, generous, and unwavering in their support. They offered to have me over for dinner every week and even insisted on driving me to and from chemotherapy treatments on Wednesdays. At the time, I didn't fully grasp how much their kindness would mean to me. I simply accepted their generosity with gratitude, not realizing the worst of my treatment was still ahead.

Just as my friend from flight school had saved me during a critical moment, here I was again, being rescued by the kindness of another friend and her family.

As September arrived, I cautiously looked ahead to starting my sixth and final cycle of chemotherapy. I remained optimistic about my future, holding on to the hope that I could return to the navy as a pilot. But in 1999, it was virtually unheard of for pilots diagnosed with cancer to resume flying. Faced with this harsh reality, I turned my thoughts toward what might come next. Having detached from the squadron in July, I no longer had the support to guide me through the process of negotiating my follow-on orders. From that point on, I faced the daunting task of navigating this impossible journey alone.

While in the hospital, I managed to track down the Aero-medical Reference and Waiver Guide and discovered that a waiver was possible for pilots who had completed treatment for stages I and IIA Hodgkin's disease, as long as there was no evidence of recurrence for at least two years. Since my diagnosis was stage IIA, that meant that I wasn't completely disqualified from flying. The odds were slim, but they weren't zero. There was a chance, however slim, that I could return to flying. A glimmer of hope was enough. It gave me something to hold onto, something to fight for, even if I was the underdog. Maybe, just maybe, I could find that one path to return to flying.

To turn that slim possibility into a reality, I needed to find a duty station that would allow me to complete the mandatory two-year waiting period while also giving me an opportunity to rebuild, both physically and mentally. I was in uncharted territory and knew that I had to drive this process if there was any chance for success.

With that in mind, I reached out to the navy detailer, determined to secure an assignment that would keep me moving forward. After our discussion and weighing my options, I set my sights on the Naval Postgraduate School in Monterey, California, where I could pursue a master's degree. It was the perfect fit, a place where I could heal, regain my strength, and gain the most from these next two years.

By the time I reached my sixth cycle and eleventh chemotherapy treatment, I felt a deep sense of gratitude for my friend's parents. Every Wednesday, they took time out of their schedules to drive me to and from the hospital. The nausea had become unbearable, so the nurses began giving me Ativan before treatment to help reduce sickness and increase sedation. Now, I spent my treatment lying in a bed, drifting in and out of consciousness, instead of sitting in those beautiful light blue chairs where I had spent so many grueling hours.

The nausea persisted throughout the week, often leaving me confined to my apartment bathroom. In a thoughtful gesture, my friend gifted me a small brown stuffed dog, a simple but deeply meaningful gift that brought unexpected comfort during an otherwise miserable time. That little stuffed dog became my steadfast companion, joining me on the cold bathroom floor during my worst bouts with nausea. And since every dog needs a name, I decided on "Farley the Chemo Dog," a tribute to Chris Farley, whose humor always made me laugh, and a fitting nod to my current situation.

I was rapidly losing weight, unable to keep most food down, and even when I was hungry, I had little desire to eat. In my search for something that wouldn't upset my stomach, I stumbled upon McDonald's French fries. They were the only food that seemed to create a happy environment for my stomach. And if nausea did strike, they were also the only food that tasted exactly the same coming back up as they did going down, which was the most important part of eating.

The finish line was finally within reach, with only one more chemotherapy treatment to go. As I headed to my appointment to review my latest CT scan with the doctor, both anticipation and anxiety intertwined. But rather than bracing for the worst, which is what I usually do, I felt a rare urge of excitement, ready to be done and unable to imagine any other outcome. Expecting there to be no further reduction in the size of the mediastinal mass and scattered lymph node tumors, I would be finished with chemotherapy in just a few weeks. For the past six months, my world had revolved around this goal of six cycles and twelve treatments. It was all I had known, all I had thought about, and now, the end was finally in sight.

If ever there was a punch that knocked me flat on my back, it was the moment when the doctor said there was a noticeable continued reduction in the mass, so we would need to continue treatment. In an instant, every ounce of hope, determination, and optimism drained from my body and walked right out of that room. I was absolutely devastated. I had been so certain, so ready for the finish line, that I'd gone against everything I'd known. Not only was I angry with myself that I hadn't braced for the worst, but mentally, I wasn't sure I had the strength to push through any more treatments. I looked down at the obliterated veins in my forearms, wondering if there were enough left to complete another cycle.

Then my treatment hit an unexpected fork in the road. Out of nowhere, the doctor proposed that I complete the six cycles of chemotherapy as planned, then transition to radiation treatment to specifically target the mediastinal mass. It was the only tumor that had shown further reduction in my last CT scan, meaning it likely still contained cancerous cells. I sat there, stunned for a moment, trying to process the doctor's words.

On one hand, I knew radiation would destroy everything in its path, including my lung tissue, a terrifying prospect since I wanted to return to running and triathlons and needed all the lung capacity I could manage. On the other hand, I would give anything in the world to be finished with chemotherapy and never step foot into that treatment room again. In that moment, I felt trapped between two impossible choices, each carrying its own risks and each demanding a sacrifice I wasn't ready to make.

To this day, I still can't fully explain what compelled me to make the more difficult choice, but I'm certain that it saved my life. With conviction, I voiced my disagreement with the doctor regarding radiation, arguing that while radiation targeted the mass, there could still be cancerous cells lurking in other lymph nodes, growing unnoticed while we focused solely on the mass. I insisted that chemotherapy was working—I knew we were on the right path and needed to stay the course with chemotherapy.

To my surprise, the doctor did not push back. Instead, he acknowledged my concerns and accepted my decision, adjusting my treatment plan accordingly. He explained that chemotherapy would be extended to eight cycles, now sixteen total treatments, four more than originally planned. But as the reality of those additional cycles set in, doubt crept in, and I had serious concerns about making it through the additional four treatments.

The doctor also cautioned that eight cycles were the absolute maximum amount of ABVD chemotherapy the body could endure. The toxicity posed a severe risk of extensive and lasting internal damage to the heart valves, lungs, and other vital organs. If further treatment was necessary beyond chemo, the next step would be a bone marrow transplant. I couldn't even begin to understand what that would mean if we arrived at that decision. All I knew was that if I could endure this extended regimen, I would finish by early December, just in time to begin classes at the Naval Postgraduate School in January. I just couldn't afford another unexpected twist in this journey.

After completing the sixth cycle, my mental health was declining rapidly, mirroring the deterioration of my physical health. Recalling memories and familiar facts had become increasingly difficult, and the mental fog of "chemo brain" was impossible to ignore. Simple memory recall became difficult, and this was magnified as I began studying for the GRE in preparation for graduate school and earning a master's degree.

To help with unfamiliar words, I purchased a dictionary, hoping to reinforce my vocabulary. But as I studied, I realized I was struggling to recall certain words I had once known well before chemotherapy. To track this unsettling pattern, I marked a small dot next to each word I had to look up. At first, it seemed like a useful system, but it soon became alarming when I revisited words later in my studies and found dots already beside them. Time and again, I looked up the same words, yet I had no recollection of having done so before. The evidence was there—chemotherapy was not only impacting my mind but also the process of how I stored and recalled memories and information.

Along with the mental fog, transitioning from thought to speech became an unexpected and deeply frustrating challenge. During conversations, I could clearly see a word in my mind that I wanted to say, but I found myself completely unable to speak it. Panicked, I would scramble for a similar word to replace it, desperate to keep the conversation flowing. The mental gymnastics required, not only to hold a conversation but also to anticipate and navigate these sudden roadblocks, were utterly exhausting. Beyond the frustration of these speech disfluencies, the substitute words I grasped for didn't always carry the same meaning or fit properly, leading to confusion for the listener and embarrassment for me. This struggle was a constant reminder of how much I was battling mentally each day and the cognitive toll chemotherapy had taken on me.

A few days before the start of the seventh cycle, I woke one morning, seriously wondering if I was alive or dead. The only conclusion I could draw was that I was still alive because if I were dead, my body wouldn't hurt that much. I reflected on the things I wanted to do before I started the next cycle, knowing my mobility, already limited by extreme nausea and weakened physical strength, would only worsen in the months ahead. On an impulse, I made the spontaneous decision to drive up to Niagara Falls. I had never seen the falls before and felt a desperate need to see them, perhaps for the simple reason that I wanted to experience something beautiful before my time expired.

I left early in the morning, feeling surprisingly okay, and drove the seven hours to Niagara Falls. As I parked my truck and began strolling along the river toward the falls, I allowed myself to admire the surrounding beauty, listening to the calming sound of the flowing water. When I reached the falls, the deep rumble and powerful roar vibrated through the air. The sight was equally awe-inspiring, with the mist rising and the veil of water cascading down in a stunning display of raw power and beauty. The scene was larger than life, offering me a way ahead.

It was an unexpected, impulsive decision that led me to this unforgettable place. Standing there before the roaring falls, I realized that there was something greater out there that I had yet to achieve. The sheer power and majesty of the falls became a reminder that no matter how overwhelming the struggle might become, I had to keep pushing forward. In that moment, I vowed that no matter what, I would give everything I could to keep on keepin' on.

I stayed for about thirty minutes, silently absorbing the sight and sound of the falls. Then, with a deep breath, I turned back toward the parking lot, once again enjoying the quiet, flowing sound of the river that led to the incredible roar of the falls as I walked to my truck. I hopped in my truck and sat there for a moment, just enjoying every last second of my time at the falls before the drive home. It had been a long, arduous day, but in those few moments at the falls, I found a glimmer of hope, a fleeting but powerful reminder that there was still something worth fighting for on this impossible journey.

The morning of my thirteenth treatment, I gazed into the bathroom mirror, barely recognizing the frail, bald, and oddly orange figure staring back at me. Fatigue weighed heavy, but Farley the Chemo Dog sat perched on top of the toilet, a comforting presence to converse with. Summoning every bit of effort to step over the edge of the tub and into the shower, I began my morning, bracing for yet another grueling day ahead.

Tuesday nights remained the most challenging, filled with dread as I braced myself for the pain and nausea that were sure to follow the next day. The Ativan helped by reducing the nausea and increasing the sedation during the treatment, but it also played tricks on my mind. I questioned my memories, unsure if they were dreams or fragments of actual experiences. Each day felt like a blur, and I became fixated on reaching the end of this ordeal in the quickest way possible, barely acknowledging the small, precious moments in between.

My eighth and final cycle began on Wednesday, November 17, 1999. Only two treatments remained, yet I couldn't comprehend the idea of an end to this relentless routine. Since early May, I had been living the same grueling cycle, and the thought of walking out of that hospital for the last time felt almost unimaginable. I had been trapped in this battle for so long that I couldn't imagine life beyond it. The reality of stepping into the next phase of this journey, free from the daily challenges that had defined my existence, was difficult to picture.

My memories of those final weeks were faint and elusive. I clung to the hope that if I could endure just a little longer, chemotherapy would soon be behind me. And if, by some miracle, I was able to survive and make it out of this diabolical nightmare, I would need to pack all of my apartment into my truck, drive to Jacksonville, Florida, collect my belongings that the squadron had brought back from Puerto Rico, then continue to Monterey, California, to find a place to live and start graduate school in early January.

The road ahead felt distant and insurmountable, a challenge I couldn't quite bring myself to face. Officially, I was still a navy pilot, but in reality, I felt disconnected and like I was no longer a part of the navy. I felt abandoned in this alternate world, left stranded in an unfamiliar existence and forced to navigate my uncertain future alone.

There were just enough viable veins remaining in my arms to get me through my final treatment on December 1, 1999. The once prominent, rope-like veins that had lined my forearms had all hardened and disappeared from the assault of chemotherapy. Left behind were only needle scars and thin, bare, weakened forearms. By the time of my final Wednesday blood draw, there were no accessible veins left in my arms. The nurse had to carefully search and settle on using a vein from the back of my hand. A painful reminder that would remain with me every day for the rest of my life, as the veins in my arm would never return, and every single future blood draw would come from a small, fragile vein in the back of my hand.

I completed my final CT scan and met with the doctor to review the results on December 12, 1999. I felt concerned when the doctor entered the room with a stoic look, expecting him to enter with a large smile and good news. Because of this, I braced myself for the worst but still hoped for the best, knowing with absolute certainty that my body could not endure further treatment.

I was both shocked and relieved when the doctor informed me that the last two CT scans had shown no change, officially marking the end of chemotherapy and the beginning of remission. After eight of the most brutal months of my life, I had finally reached the end. But instead of the triumph I had expected, the moment felt strangely anticlimactic.

The doctor handed me my discharge paperwork, told me I was free to go, and left the room. There was no discussion of follow-up care and no plan for what came next. I simply gathered my things, walked out of the hospital toward my truck, and drove away. There was no bell to ring, no one to hug, and no triumphant moment to mark the end of my battle. In the absence of any grand announcement that I had beaten cancer, at least for now, I simply walked out of the hospital nauseous, frail, exhausted, and unnoticed, just like any other day.

Just because I had completed chemotherapy didn't mean that I suddenly felt great or regained any discernible strength. The toll of eight grueling months weighed heavily on me, both mentally and physically. It would probably take another eight months or more before I could find my way back to some kind of new normal. The drive across the country was the only time I had to prepare and start to recover since I had to be ready to begin graduate school in early January. My body would eventually rebuild and rejuvenate, but I still needed to figure out a way to accomplish that. As for the mental fog of "chemo brain" that lingered, I expected recovery to be a much longer journey, one that I wasn't sure I would ever fully navigate.

CHAPTER V

The cross-country drive proved to be far more challenging than anticipated. After a brief stop in Jacksonville to collect the belongings I'd left in Puerto Rico, I pressed on westward. With little appetite and frequent bouts of nausea forcing emergency stops, the journey was slow, exhausting, and isolating. Only Farley the Chemo Dog was there to provide me with company. Lacking the energy for long stretches behind the wheel, each mile felt like a struggle. Seeking some connection, I used my cell phone, which was very spotty in coverage back then, to make some calls and reached out to college friends living in San Diego, asking if I could crash at their place for a couple of days before heading to Monterey.

My nausea had eased during the week-long journey, allowing me to eat somewhat normally again. However, regaining strength and the nearly thirty pounds I had lost would take time. After months of associating food with nausea and discomfort, I had unconsciously trained myself to avoid eating altogether. As a result, I struggled to distinguish between hunger and nausea, turning every meal into a frustrating process of trial and error, both in food choices and portion sizes. Relearning how to eat again was more challenging and frustrating than I had expected.

Slowly making my way, I finally arrived in San Diego, where the smiling faces and hugs from friends provided a much-needed reprieve from the isolation of the past few months. Though the sudden burst of activity was overwhelming at times, it felt great to have actual conversations again and gauge where my mental capacity and strength stood now that chemotherapy was behind me. What seemed like just a few days with friends was, in reality, a significant step forward in discovering what life after cancer would be like. Grateful for their kindness, I set off for Monterey.

Monterey proved to be the perfect place for a fresh start, and I was eager to begin graduate school, immersing myself in academics. It felt like a second chance, an opportunity to move beyond the disappointment and heartbreak of my collapsed lung and the less-than-ideal end to my undergraduate years. My mental sharpness returned fairly quickly, though not with the same precision and clarity I'd had before chemotherapy. A persistent fog lingered, something I would have to learn to navigate, reshaping the way I received, processed, and communicated information.

Regaining my physical strength, however, proved to be a much slower process. After settling into my new apartment in the new year, I attempted my first run in what felt like forever. My only goal was to jog slowly around the block, just a third of a mile. Halfway through, my body gave out, and I collapsed. Exhausted, I walked the rest of the way home, taking a few sitting breaks along the way. It was clear that I had a long road ahead and would need to rebuild my strength from the ground up.

The first quarter of school felt like a refresher in undergraduate engineering, which eased my transition back into academics. I was placed in the combat systems science and technology curriculum, leading to a degree in applied physics. Although I had hoped to pursue mechanical engineering, pilots weren't typically allowed in that program. After several conversations with my advisor and a bit of persistent lobbying on my part, we found a workaround: I could complete the full physics curriculum, take five additional engineering courses, and write a thesis in engineering to ultimately earn the degree I wanted. I would just have to calculate how I would fit those extra courses into an already-packed schedule.

My classmates were friendly, and the campus was both beautiful and calming, exactly what I needed. Of course, arriving with a bald head and no eyebrows sparked some curiosity, so I came up with a few funny cancer stories to share. I hadn't really thought about how I would explain such a grueling experience, but I knew I didn't want my classmates to see me as someone seeking sympathy. Humor seemed like the best way to lighten the conversation and put everyone at ease, including myself.

By mid-January, my hair finally began to grow back, though, to my surprise, the first stubble was orange and curly. Having always had straight light brown hair, I could only hope this was a temporary effect. I suspected the Adriamycin chemo had dyed my hair follicles the same way it had tinted my skin and turned my urine orange. I wasn't quite ready to embrace this new look, and after a few millimeters of curly orange hair, my appearance slowly returned to normal.

As I progressed through the class syllabus, my focus shifted to meeting with the school's flight surgeon to schedule an examination and submit a package to the navy medical board. During chemotherapy, I'd been placed on limited duty due to my condition. Now, in remission and with treatment completed, I needed a medical board to officially determine that my health was restored and that I was fit to return to full duty. This was especially important because I was scheduled to advance to the next rank of lieutenant (O-3) on June 1, and that promotion could only happen if I was no longer on limited duty.

The next few months were challenging as I navigated the uncertainty surrounding my medical future. I found a local oncology doctor to conduct the examination, a crucial step in advancing my medical board process. Unlike the minimal guidance I'd received upon leaving Bethesda, this doctor provided clear direction, explaining that I would need examinations every three months for the first two years, every six months for the following three years, then annually thereafter. While I was grateful for the clarity, I realized these examinations would be excruciating—I would be getting frequent chest X-rays, and blood would now and forever have to be drawn from the veins in the back of my hands due to the devastation to the veins in my arms.

With my first follow-up exam complete, my medical board process began, but it presented an unexpected challenge. At Bethesda, my limited duty medical board had been practically automatic, a standard practice for hospitalized military members. However, at the Naval Postgraduate School, securing a medical board for a post-cancer patient seeking a return to full duty proved far more complicated. Once again, I was forced to navigate my navy career alone. No one on staff had experience handling military medical boards for students, leaving me to manage the entire process without prior knowledge or guidance, all while balancing the demands of a rigorous academic workload.

I remained very close with my dad, and we spoke more often than we had during my chemotherapy. He was excited about his new job and the fresh start he had found with his new girlfriend, and his positivity was infectious. I shared in his enthusiasm, but beneath the surface, I grappled with doubts about my future and uncertainty about where my life was heading. I never told him, nor anyone, about the challenges and pain I had endured during chemotherapy treatment. Instead, I simply maintained the appearance of positivity and optimism, even during the toughest times. Despite everything happening in my life, his phone calls were a comforting reconnection to family, another welcome contrast to the isolation I had felt throughout treatment.

I had finally built up enough strength and stamina to complete my run around the block and was ready to take on more physical activities. I began rollerblading along the Monterey boardwalk regularly to strengthen my legs and core, and I joined local triathlon and bike racing teams, which reignited my passion for swimming, biking, and running. While my strength was still a far cry from where it had been before chemotherapy, I was determined, worked hard, and made steady progress.

I completed my first quarter of school and thoroughly enjoyed the academic challenge, feeling very optimistic about my progress. It was refreshing to face a challenge that was both positive and rewarding. Though the lingering mental fog remained, I was learning to navigate its barriers, gradually improving my ability to process and recall information more quickly. Every question, conversation, and memory recall remained a challenge, but I was adapting to my new normal. I came to accept that the days of effortlessly visualizing textbook pages or instantly recalling word spellings and definitions were a thing of the past. Chemo brain was here to stay, and I needed to find a state of equilibrium, somewhere between frustration and acceptance.

The persistent aches and pains in my chest continued to worry me, with moments when the pain was so intense that dread and anxiety consumed my thoughts. My second oncologist visit was still a month away, but the fear of what the X-rays and blood work might reveal never left me. To keep my mind occupied, I continued to focus on academics and my persistent return to athletics. Each time I felt chest pain, I would just go for a short run. They were not long or fast, but I was running again, keeping my mind positive through the uncertainty.

One week into my second quarter of school, I was feeling a bit stronger and eating healthier than I had in a long time. It was Sunday, April 9, 2000, a day that felt perfect, with the kind of weather Monterey was known for. After returning from my usual morning bike ride, I was surprised to see a red blinking light on my answering machine. I pressed play and heard my mom's voice, trembling with tears, asking me to call her back as soon as possible. A wave of unease swept over me.

As I dialed the phone, I braced myself for bad news, but nothing could have prepared me for what I was about to hear.

My mom's first words were, "Your dad is gone," and I collapsed to the floor. A flood of questions filled my mind, but I was frozen in silence and disbelief. I thought that was the worst of it, until she added, "He took his own life." My entire body went completely numb and silent. The world around me faded, and if my mom said another word, I didn't hear it. I managed to tell her I would call her back, hung up the phone, and lay on the floor, staring at nothing for quite a while, trying to comprehend the unimaginable. A billion questions raced through my mind, yet not a single one had an answer.

Throughout the years, in every conversation and moment spent with my dad, he never hinted at any despair. There were no signals, no signs, and no warnings that he was struggling with anything, and I never saw this coming. He was the type of person who, if he was having an issue, would jump into his car and drive to visit me. After three months of rebuilding my life and finally feeling a sense of progress after cancer, it was as if I had been violently yanked right back into the pit of despair and misery once again.

After an undetermined amount of time passed, I forced myself up from the floor, finally able to shower and change out of my biking clothes. I must have stood in the shower for an hour or so, lifeless and lost in thought. Unaware of the time, I eventually got dressed and ate some much-needed food. Once my mind cleared enough, I grabbed the yellow pages and began looking for a flight back to Wisconsin.

While my memory remains cloudy, I recall meeting with the pastor along with my family to coordinate the details of the wake and funeral. On the day of the wake, I stood at the front of the church for hours, greeting each person who came to pay their respects, the line stretching out of the church and down the sidewalk. The excitement of seeing friends and family that I hadn't seen in many years was exciting, yet the pain of the moment left me feeling distraught, unable to find any words that were appropriate at the moment. It was a long, difficult day.

On the day of the funeral, my uncles brought the horse-drawn open carriage from the farm to carry the casket from the church to the graveyard. As I stood just inside the church, waiting for the pallbearers to assemble, I held a set of pilot wings in my hand. Turning to the funeral director, I handed them over and asked that he place them on Dad's chest. It was my way of honoring him, a symbol of appreciation for his unwavering support and the inspiration that had carried me through life's toughest challenges. Without him, I wouldn't have had the strength to fight, to endure, to be alive and present in that very moment.

It was a beautiful April day, unusually warm with the sunlight casting a serene glow. The horse-drawn carriage sat beautifully at the bottom of the church steps. The perfect tribute to my dad, who had always loved horses and the farm. It had been the family's idea, and it couldn't have been more fitting. The sidewalk and street overflowed with people, a testament to the profound impact he'd had on so many lives. As the casket was carefully loaded and the procession began, everyone walked alongside the carriage for the quarter-mile journey to the graveyard. That slow walk felt endless, the longest and most excruciating journey I have ever made.

Returning to Monterey after the funeral, I felt numb and unmotivated. The weight of unanswered questions lingered, and the image of my dad's headstone haunted my thoughts, never leaving my mind. I was enveloped in a fog of confusion and thrust back into a world that hadn't paused, even though mine had come to a halt. The academic schedule continued, as did everything else, but inside, I was still trying to make sense of the hollow space and crushing grief.

A handful of weeks later, I kept a promise to attend a friend's wedding in Las Vegas—something I might've normally declined. But standing in that neon blur of celebration, surrounded by friends, laughter, heartfelt toasts, and an awkward bachelor party, I found a moment of stillness. It wasn't an escape. It was an awakening: the subtle but undeniable reminder that life continues, that joy and sorrow can sit quietly side by side.

I returned to Monterey, finished my second quarter, and earned a strong GPA. I also completed and submitted my medical board package for consideration and approval. I was promoted to lieutenant (O-3) on time, feeling both unprepared and strangely ready to tackle the next year and a half of graduate school.

Looking back, I found strength and determination in a time and place where there was no discernable way to escape. My memories from Monterey and that period are clouded and conflicted. I can't quite recall what gave me the strength to continue fighting after years of relentless challenges. But one thing became clear: Those challenges had changed everything about me, both physically and mentally. I wasn't entirely sure who I was in that moment, but I was figuring it out, and being in grad school was the best place and opportunity to do just that.

In the midst of all that searching, I drove up to Lake Tahoe to meet the same friend who had helped me through chemo with her family. I didn't need to explain much—our history was written in hospital chairs and IV drips. We sat overlooking the snow-covered lake, wrapped in cold air and quiet understanding. We didn't talk about death, or fear, or even the weight of it all, but it was all there—unspoken and shared. That weekend gave me something I hadn't realized I needed: permission to exist without a mask, to be scarred yet still moving forward.

When Christmas arrived, I felt the pull of home in a different way. I flew back to be with family, unsure how it would feel to be at the farm without Dad. The holiday was quieter than usual. There were fewer jokes, less noise. But there was love—steady and warm. I found comfort in the ritual of being together, even with the empty space where he should have been. That visit reminded me that grief doesn't just fade—it folds itself into tradition, into memory, into the way we gather and continue.

A year had passed since Dad's death when Easter rolled around. I invited a few close friends to spend the weekend with me in Monterey. There wasn't much of a plan beyond that—just the need for familiar faces and a taste of normal. We wandered the city, stumbled into good food and better conversations, and let the days stretch out in that effortless way that only old friends can manage. At sunset, we drove to the coast and watched the sun melt into the Pacific, taking in all the beauty that Monterey had to offer. It wasn't a grand gesture or some kind of breakthrough, but it mattered. In the middle of everything I couldn't control, I had chosen to open my door, to let people in, and to let life feel light again, even just for a little while. That, more than anything, felt like progress.

With only eight months until graduation, my thoughts about flying in the navy were rekindled. It was 2001, and the commercial technology industry was booming. I found myself thinking more about finding a way out of the navy and using this newfound knowledge and experience in mechanical engineering to transition into the private sector. But then I thought of my dad and the pride I'd seen on his face the day I'd left for flight school. Deep down, I knew that I had come so far, overcoming challenges I'd never imagined, and I couldn't let go of the dream. I had to keep fighting for my childhood aspiration that had driven me this far, encouraging me to return to the skies as a navy pilot.

My physical strength had returned to a respectable level, though my lungs had yet to fully regain their efficiency before the collapse and chemotherapy. I was racing more triathlons and prioritizing fitness daily, but my body still struggled as I grappled with what my new normal would be physically. One day, during a training swim in Monterey Bay, as sea lions playfully nibbled at our toes and glided alongside us, I had an idea: Perhaps a long triathlon race might offer the time, space, and clarity I needed to reflect on my path forward and future in the navy.

I registered for my first half Ironman, the Wildflower Triathlon, held in San Luis Obispo on May 5, 2001. Naturally, it was Cinco de Mayo, which meant the possibility of a few celebratory Mexican beers post-race. But before I could earn that celebration, the race had something to teach me.

Another incredible chapter in my journey was about to unfold, though I had no idea. Clad in my wetsuit, swim cap, and goggles, I stood at the edge of the water, ready for the beach start and the 1.2-mile swim. My age group's heat was lined up under the iconic Wildflower inflatable arch, each of us sweating inside our wetsuits, hearts pounding in anticipation as we waited for the start.

The gun fired, and I sprinted toward the lake. Fueled by excitement about my improved physical condition, I swam way too fast, burning through energy I'd need later. By the time I reached the shore, I was completely exhausted, with the bike ride and run still ahead. As I jogged out of the water toward transition one, my foot slipped on the slick, algae-covered boat ramp, sending a sharp jolt of pain through my left big toe as it slammed into the concrete.

At transition one, my toe throbbed with pain as I struggled to put on my socks and bike shoes for the grueling fifty-six-mile ride. I strapped on my bike helmet and sunglasses, grabbed my bike from the stand, and jogged toward the transition exit. Each step sent waves of pain shooting up my foot. I hadn't even mounted the bike yet and had doubts that I could even start the run, let alone finish the race. The course was both hilly and windy, and the exhaustion from the swim weighed heavily on me. Still, I pressed on, determined to keep moving forward, the rhythmic hum of the aero wheels and the wind rushing through my helmet providing a steady focus. My toe hurt, but with minimal impact, I was maintaining a decent pace, though I certainly wasn't breaking any Wildflower speed records that day.

I reached transition two, dismounted my bike, and felt a sharp, searing pain shoot through my foot. I didn't dare remove my sock, fearing what I might see, opting instead to simply swap shoes and braced myself for the 13.1-mile run ahead. The course was desert-hot and hilly, and I drifted in and out of a euphoric haze, my thoughts consumed by the relentless throbbing in my toe. Not once did I reflect on my navy future as I had originally intended.

Halfway through the run, I realized it would be a fight to the finish. I was running on empty, completely drained of energy. Soon, the feeling in my legs began to fade, replaced by cold sweats and numbness creeping in. The temptation to cut the course, to give up and collapse into the bed of my truck, rip off my shoes, and sink into sleep was almost overpowering. But I knew that I could never live with the shame of giving up that easily. I forced myself to reframe the moment, telling myself, *This is just a run, about forty-five more minutes of discomfort. I've spent more time than that just staring at a clock in the ugliest light blue chair you've ever seen, enduring far worse pain than this.*

Digging deep, summoning every fragment of energy and willpower, the lyrics to Bon Jovi's *Living on a Prayer* somehow materialized in my mind on full repeat. This became my mantra, not just to get me through the race but also to push me forward in life. I was running on fumes, barely staying hydrated but managing to consume just enough water when it was available. Then, finally, mile marker 12, then 13. The finish line was in sight.

I fell across the finish line with a respectable time. The relief of an ice-cold wet towel on the back of my neck was indescribable, and a kind volunteer assisted me in my forward stumble out of the exit chute to where I collapsed ungracefully onto the ground. Lying there, staring at the sky, I let the weight of the race settle over me. After a few moments of reflection,

I forced myself up and made my way to the lake. Peeling off my shoe and sock, I dipped my foot into the cold water, only to be horrified by the sight of my big toe, swollen and purple, resembling a small eggplant.

That night, camping on-site with my triathlon teammates, I celebrated Cinco de Mayo with a few well-earned beers, smiling with pride, knowing I had fought through every urge to quit. Though I hadn't spent the race contemplating my navy future as planned, I had learned something more valuable, and the beers had never tasted so good. My toe healed in time, and I raced again, this time being much smarter about pacing myself in the swim. Looking back, that race was more than just a test of endurance; it was a lesson in resilience in the face of struggle, one that would stay with me throughout my career.

Spending my last summer in Monterey, I was determined to make the most of an amazing opportunity I never could have imagined before my cancer diagnosis. The rigor of academics was mounting, and choosing a thesis topic only added to the stress. Searching for a reprieve from anxiety, I made it a priority to spend more time outdoors on my bike, soaking in the sights and sounds of Pebble Beach, 17-Mile Drive, and the sweeping expanse of Monterey Bay.

Tuesday night "crits" quickly became the highlight of my week. I'd join my Velo Club Monterey teammates to race a criterium on a closed circuit in Fort Ord, bikes flying through tight corners at high speeds, with sprints and tactical positioning moves to keep the adrenaline high. On the other days, I'd head out for evening runs when the air cooled and the breeze off the bay made everything feel just right. To wrap up the week, I'd plunge into the frigid waters of Monterey Bay for

Friday afternoon swims, the fifty-four-degree ocean serving as all the motivation I needed to swim faster.

Knowing that I might never return to this paradise, I couldn't help but feel a strange sense of gratitude for the path that had led me here, even if that path had begun with a Hodgkin's lymphoma diagnosis. Hidden within the struggle of recovery was a gift: the chance to experience this little slice of heaven where my healing became something deeper, shaped by moments of peace, adrenaline, and connection.

With the final quarter of school underway, my focus shifted primarily to researching and writing a thesis as the submission deadline fast approached. In rare quiet moments, I found myself reflecting on how far I'd come since arriving. That first failed run around the block felt like a distant memory, a stark contrast to the strength I had built alongside teammates who had become a vital part of the journey. As my time in Monterey came to a close, a sense of sadness settled in, knowing that this chapter was ending and that I might never cross paths with any of my new friends again.

Before my stint in Monterey ended, I had one final triathlon to race. I registered for the Triathlon at Pacific Grove, scheduled for Saturday, September 15, 2001. This race would be my pinnacle moment, a chance to prove to myself just how much I had improved physically over the past two years. As a local event, the logistics were simple, and, best of all, it was the very course I had been training on. The chance to race one last time alongside my amazing teammates made it all the more meaningful.

It was the Tuesday before the race, and as always on Tuesdays, we wore uniforms to class. Dressed in my summer white uniform, I was just about to walk out the door when my phone rang. My friend's voice was urgent and tense, telling me to turn on the TV and to stay home since the base was on lockdown. It was September 11, 2001. I stood frozen in my apartment living room, watching in disbelief as tragedy unfolded.

In the wake of the national devastation, there was uncertainty about whether the triathlon would be canceled. I really needed this race more than ever, but I understood why it might not be the right time. If it were postponed, I could only hope to still be in Monterey when it was rescheduled. On Thursday, the announcement came, and the triathlon would proceed as planned. With the weight of recent events heavy on my mind, I knew I couldn't approach this race the same way. It had to mean something more. I needed to do something different, something patriotic, to honor this moment of my final race in this beautiful place.

The day before the race, I purchased a small seventeen-by-twelve-inch American flag mounted on a wooden dowel. On race morning, I secured it to the back of my bike seat and attached my race number, 144, to the frame. I was focused and ready to race. I knew the flag would flap proudly behind me during the ride, creating extra resistance, but I didn't care. It was a symbol of something far greater than the race itself.

Just before the race began, we gathered for the traditional playing of the national anthem. On opposite cliffs in Pacific Grove, two lines of buglers stood facing one another, silhouetted against the morning sky. They began to play *Taps* in a haunting call-and-response, the notes echoing across the bay like a solemn conversation carried on the wind. The sound lingered over the water, reverberating through the crowd and settling into a silence more powerful than words. It was unlike anything I had ever experienced—moving, reverent, unforgettable. There wasn't a dry eye in sight.

When the music faded, the applause erupted, rolling across the bay and straight into the heart of the crowd. A surge of pride and adrenaline swept over us, electric, unspoken, and understood by everyone there. The early morning quiet roared to life, and you could feel the collective energy shift. The best part of the day was still ahead, and we all knew it.

I sauntered back to my assigned spot in the transition area, walking slowly, deep in thought. I surveyed my setup, helmet, shoes, and race belt, making sure that everything was exactly where it needed to be. I gave my bike tires a quick squeeze; they felt firm, just right. My hands moved with muscle memory as my mind walked through each transition, one step at a time. Swim to bike. Bike to run. I wasn't nervous, just focused. Ready!

As my wave's start time approached, I lined up, swim cap pulled tight, goggles secure, wetsuit zipped up, and ready to race. When the starting gun cracked through the early morning air, I surged forward, the frigid cold bite of the water snapping me fully into race mode. This time, I paced myself, drawing from hard lessons learned in past races. No frantic splashing, no wasted energy. Just smooth, steady strokes.

The 1.5-kilometer swim course was unlike any other triathlon. It followed a two-loop course through the kelp beds of Monterey Bay, winding past the seals, sea lions, and the occasional sea otter gliding on by like a silent spectator. After the first loop, I exited the water, ran barefoot around a massive rock on the beach, and dove headfirst back into the bay for the final loop. It was wild, raw, beautiful, and frigid cold.

I emerged from the water with a solid time and sprinted toward the transition area, peeling off my wetsuit as I ran. Every move felt automatic, goggles and wetsuit tossed aside, bike shoes on, helmet buckled. I grabbed my bike from the rack, wheeled it to the mount line, and clipped in. The moment my shoes locked into the pedals, I surged forward with a burst of energy like never before.

Proudly carrying the American flag behind me, I blasted down the course. The bike course followed a looped route, giving spectators four chances to see us fly by as we worked our way around the forty-kilometer circuit. The road twisted and turned, with the town on one side and the vast, shimmering horizon of Monterey Bay on the other. The pavement was smooth and fast, and the breeze off the bay was cool and refreshing. The cheers along the sidelines grew louder with every lap, and each pass felt like another shot of adrenaline propelling me forward.

As I entered the final loop, my mind shifted to the run, mentally rehearsing how I wanted to finish strong. I rolled up to the dismount line, jumped off the bike, and jogged into transition two. I racked my bike, swapped into my running shoes, and grabbed my race belt. After taking one last gulp from my water bottle, my gaze landed on the American flag still attached to my bike. In that instant, a thought struck me, clear and sudden. Without hesitation, I grabbed the flag and headed out of transition, ready to tackle the final ten-kilometer run.

I felt another surge of energy, my legs moving faster than I had ever anticipated. As I made my way through the course, the pavement shifted beneath me, from smooth, fast stretches to cobblestone streets winding through the town. The crowd was thick, their cheers echoing off the buildings, fueling my momentum. The American flag, firmly gripped in my hand, was even more special that day; it was a symbol to everyone. To me, it represented pride and deep commitment to myself, and it propelled me forward.

The route curved through Monterey, taking me past familiar sights and landmarks, the energy soaking into my stride. As I hit the final stretch, the finish line came into view, and I gave everything I had left. It was a pinnacle moment, one where I refused to leave anything on the course. I crossed the line fourth in my age group, with a time of 2:14:47, missing the podium by just under a minute.

The next day, Sunday morning, I met up with my teammates for our usual bike ride, planning to treat it as a recovery ride after the race. But that day would turn out to be unlike any other. As we gathered at our usual spot in downtown Monterey, I noticed one of my teammates sitting off to the side, reading the newspaper. It struck me as rather unusual, but I didn't think much of it at first.

Then he walked over to me, holding the paper out in front of him. I couldn't shake the sensation that everyone else knew something that I didn't. I felt that something was off, and panic slowly began to rise within me. He handed me the paper and said that it was for me. I politely replied that I didn't usually read the paper and certainly didn't have anywhere to put it during our bike ride. But he insisted, saying I should take a look at the sports section, specifically about yesterday's race.

At that moment, I was completely thrown off. Why would I care about the newspaper right now? And why was he so insistent on me reading the sports section just before we were set to head out on our ride? The urgency in his voice only deepened my confusion.

As I looked around, I realized that everyone was watching me, which only increased my anxiety. Feeling the weight of their eyes, and out of politeness, I opened the paper to the sports section, not knowing what to expect. When my gaze landed on the page, I couldn't believe my eyes. There I was—a photo of me on my bike, the American flag proudly flying behind me, splashed across the front page of the sports section.

It was an incredible gift, not just the paper itself, but as a symbol of everything I had achieved and overcome to reach that moment. Seeing that photo was a reminder of the journey, the countless hours of training, the struggles, and the unwavering belief in myself. But above all, it was a reminder of my teammates, who had stood by me every step of the way with continuous support and encouragement.

Halloween drew near, and the team had organized a big costume party. I knew this might be my last chance to see everyone outside of training events, so I decided to go. It was the perfect opportunity for me to cherish the journey we had shared and thank everyone for the lasting memories before graduation and my departure from Monterey.

I arrived late, one of the few not wearing a costume, mostly because I wanted to spend time catching up with friends and saying my goodbyes. I hadn't been there long when a girl I vaguely knew approached me, and we started talking. We chatted for quite a while before eventually being pulled away by other friends.

Throughout my time in Monterey, I had deliberately prioritized my physical and mental growth, knowing that dating would add complexity to an already-demanding routine. I had made a couple of attempts, each beginning with genuine interest, hope, and a positive connection. But somewhere between the early-morning workouts, late-night study sessions, and the emotional residue of everything else I'd been through, it had just never seemed to work.

So when my phone rang a few days after the party, and it was the girl I'd met that night, I hesitated. I hadn't expected to hear from her, and part of me wasn't sure if I was ready to dive into anything, especially given my past attempts with dating. A little uncertain at first, we spoke for hours, completely unaware of how much time had passed. The conversation flowed effortlessly, as if we'd known each other for years and were catching up. Eventually, I glanced at the clock and realized how late it was, mentioning that I should get going since I had an early-morning class. Just as I was about to say goodnight, she surprised me by asking if I'd like to go on a date that weekend.

Dating hadn't even crossed my mind during my final months in Monterey, but for the first time, I considered the possibility of letting my guard down and giving it a chance. I had been so protective and cautious, shielding the past and the pain I had endured. But then, I thought that maybe this was an opportunity to move past the heartbreak of my last serious relationship and the haunting memory of being abandoned while lying in the hospital. Something about this felt different. Maybe it was a chance to move beyond those scars, to let go of the fear of being vulnerable again. The real issue, though, was timing. Writing my thesis consumed my days, and with only two months left before graduating and heading to Jacksonville, Florida, I wasn't sure if I had space for anything more.

Anxious about the thought of dating again, I focused on calming my nerves before our first date. But when the date arrived and she accidentally dropped her drink as we talked by the firepit, I felt an unexpected sense of relief to see that she was just as nervous as I was. The night turned out to be much better than I'd anticipated, and I genuinely enjoyed our time together. Still, in the back of my mind, I had serious concerns and worries about the future and where we might be in just over a month when it came time to pack up my apartment for the move.

Given my busy academic schedule, my free time was scarce, so we settled on a quick lunch date. It felt rushed, and to my disappointment, it didn't go well. Awkward silence filled most of our time together as we struggled to find anything to talk about, which was such a contrast to our effortless first phone call. When we finished eating and went our separate ways, I was certain that this was over before it had a chance to begin, just like my previous dating attempts. In some ways, that would have made the next few months so much easier for me.

But since when have I ever done anything the easy way? A few days later, she called me and suggested we take a trip to San Francisco. She promised to take me to The Buena Vista, the world's most famous Irish coffee house. I was surprised she called after how poorly the last date had gone, but I also couldn't deny that a weekend away sounded appealing, especially after the grueling demands of putting together my thesis.

The Buena Vista was packed. We managed to order two Irish coffees and searched for a place to sit and talk. When two seats opened up across from an older couple, we politely asked if we could join them. They welcomed us with warm smiles and soon struck up a conversation. We chatted and laughed with them for a while when, out of the blue, they asked how long we'd been together. In unison, we both answered, "Two weeks." They chuckled, remarking that we looked great together, as if we'd known each other forever. At that moment, I glanced at her just as she turned to look at me, and though neither of us said a word, we both knew exactly what the other was thinking.

The date and the trip turned out far better than I had expected, and she even invited me to spend Thanksgiving with her at her parents' house. During the long six-hour drive, we talked and laughed, thoroughly enjoying each other's company. Then, in a rare departure from my usually well-planned, engineer-like nature, I spontaneously put myself out there and asked if she would move with me to Jacksonville, Florida, in a few weeks. To my surprise, she happily agreed, so we pulled over on the side of the road to take pictures and celebrate. But as we continued our journey, a new thought crossed my mind: How would I move not just one, but two apartments?

My third lesson in expectation management came subtly in early December when I visited the flight surgeon to obtain an aviation medical up-chit, allowing me to arrive in Jacksonville ready for training and flying. Having reached exactly two years since my last chemotherapy treatment on December 1, 1999, I met the waiver criteria. After reviewing my oncologist's recent examination, the flight surgeon signed the form and handed it to me. As I left his office, holding the up-chit tightly, just as I had so many years ago after my NAMI medical examination, I couldn't shake the thought that this was far too easy. After overcoming significant challenges that most navy pilots would never face, I knew that greater obstacles still lay ahead. But I pushed those thoughts aside, ignored the voice of common reason, and focused on graduation and the signed up-chit in my hand. I officially received my orders for Jacksonville, Florida, to rejoin the Pro's Nest (VP-30) squadron to begin training in the P-3C once again.

CHAPTER VI

Graduation marked a rewarding conclusion to the challenges of the past two years. Receiving the Outstanding Thesis Award was especially gratifying, a validation of the countless hours I had poured into research and writing. The ceremony was brief, but the moment carried immense significance. After enduring years of hardship, I was eager for the opportunity to reclaim the career that had been abruptly taken from me. I took a moment to reflect on how far I had come before shifting my focus forward—but not too far forward after learning from the mistakes of my past. The next adventure awaited, and I was ready and determined to embrace the future, fully aware that unknown hurdles and barriers likely lay ahead.

The drive to Jacksonville, Florida, felt entirely different than my last trip. Not only was I in a much better place, but I also had my girlfriend as company this time around. Since it was mid-December, we detoured to Wisconsin to spend the holidays with my family. Farm life was a whole new experience for a girl from California, but she embraced it and didn't bolt back home. From there, we continued to Jacksonville, found an apartment, and moved in with the belongings from my apartment. Shortly after, we flew back to Monterey to pack up her things, then hit the road once again in her vehicle, this time taking the southern route for new escapades and a bit more adventurous fun.

Upon reporting to the squadron, the pilot training team informed me that, given my limited operational flight experience and three-year absence from flying, I would need to complete the entire training syllabus again. I accepted without hesitation, feeling an overwhelming sense of excitement to be back in aviation after years of anxiety and doubt.

What I hadn't anticipated was that many of my former flight school peers, now seasoned instructors with over a thousand flight hours, would be the ones training and instructing me in the aircraft this time around. While I was thrilled to be back with familiar faces, a nagging voice in the back of my mind reminded me that this situation was not entirely positive. I was now over three years behind my year group in the navy, a reality that I feared would come back to haunt me in the future.

One day during classroom training, the squadron flight surgeon appeared at the door and called for me by name. Though we had never met, I knew exactly what this was about. As we walked to her office, my mind raced with a mix of anticipation and uncertainty. Once inside, we discussed my cancer history and current physical condition. She guided me through the waiver process, explaining that my condition required a series of additional medical tests and evaluations. The results would then be compiled into a comprehensive medical package and submitted to NAMI for review, and they would determine whether I was eligible for a waiver to resume flying. I'd known it was too good to be true when the Monterey flight surgeon had simply handed me an up-chit without any questions or concerns.

After two months of exhaustive medical tests, evaluations, and consultations, the flight surgeon reviewed the completed medical package with me before submitting it. A few weeks later, on May 7, 2002, I received a letter from the Navy Bureau of Medicine and Surgery. The letter stated that I was not physically qualified for duty involving flying and that a waiver was not recommended at that time. Once again, I was stopped in my tracks. I had fought so hard for so long, all for nothing. My mental strength and determination began to wane, worn thin by the weight of every battle that I'd endured in search of a destination that I was now unable to reach.

I was frustrated, upset, and on the verge of just giving up, wanting nothing more than to start over anywhere else, far from this place. I completely shut down and shut off for a few days, needing time to collect my thoughts. Having just moved back to Jacksonville, I couldn't help but wonder where the navy might send me and what my future would look like without flying. In my darkest moments, I struggled to understand if I was truly in control of my life or merely a passenger, swept along by circumstances with little say in where they led.

Out of nowhere, a memory surfaced, the one where I had disagreed with my oncology doctor in Bethesda about proceeding with radiation after the sixth cycle, insisting instead on continuing with chemotherapy. I wasn't sure why that memory resurfaced, but in that instant, I realized that I couldn't let others determine my future. Fueled by a mix of frustration and sheer determination, I took action. I scheduled an appointment with an oncologist to review my medical history and provide an examination report to include in a resubmitted medical package for my waiver request.

Since receiving my first disqualification letter, I was pulled from ground school training, and time was running out. I needed to submit an updated medical package quickly before the navy reassigned me somewhere else that was not aviation. Working closely with the flight surgeon, we coordinated every detail necessary for resubmission. We both knew it would take a miracle to make this happen. I was incredibly fortunate to have a flight surgeon who was proactive and dedicated to helping me through this process. For the first time in as long as I could remember, it felt like I had someone who offered support and assisted me in carrying the weight of this burden.

After submitting the new medical package, every day seemed like an eternity. I found myself staring at my phone, just waiting for it to ring, hoping for good news. Then, on May 23, 2002, the flight surgeon called me, asking me to come to the hangar—the letter that would decide my future had finally arrived. At the hangar, with a mix of dread and anticipation, I scanned the first few lines that stated I was not physically qualified for duty involving flying due to three specific medical conditions directly related to the internal damage caused by the toxicity of the chemotherapy. My heart sank. In that moment, I wanted to stop the world and step off.

But then I kept reading.

The next paragraph stated, "After review, a waiver is recommended for duty involving actual control of aircraft as a Naval Aviator, Service Group I. Waiver is contingent upon:

member remains asymptomatic and on no medication. Annual submission directed."

The navy had granted me a waiver due to my history with cancer, allowing me to return to the aircraft and flying as long as I remained in remission and submitted additional chest X-rays and blood work each year to renew the waiver.

In an instant, my overwhelming disappointment turned into pure exhilaration, the most I had felt in years. After everything I had endured and due to the reality of my medical history, I had prepared myself for the worst, never allowing myself to be overly hopeful. But now, against all odds, I was headed back to the classroom and, soon, back to the aircraft.

The training syllabus lasted eight months and was a repeat of the curriculum I had completed back in 1998, thus requiring far less studying this time around. Flying alongside old flight school friends made my return to the cockpit even more memorable. Though the effects of chemo brain still lingered and there was much more difficulty in recalling information, I was learning how to successfully navigate the challenges. Recalling information now required a completely different approach, but graduate school had helped me develop new methods and processes, like learning to read all over again.

A few months had passed, and life was steadily moving forward. My oncology checkups had now shifted to every six months, and I felt great. I had reconnected with my old bike racing team and continued to race triathlons. All the pilots in my class were fresh out of flight school and already knew each other well. I was the outsider, the new kid in school, so it took some time to get to know everyone and find my place. By now, that was kind of familiar territory. I shared stories about my chemotherapy journey and helped them grasp some of the more difficult material, especially since this was my second time through the course.

For our six-month anniversary, I took my girlfriend out to celebrate. The evening was perfect, and we strolled along the St. Johns River, the downtown Jacksonville skyline providing a stunning backdrop as night fell. Eventually, we reached Friendship Fountain, where we paused to take in the sights and talk for a while. Once again, in a rare departure from my typically well-planned, engineer-like nature, I acted on an impulse. My mind drifted back to my college days when my carefully laid plans had imploded one night as I'd lain in a hospital bed. But now, I was done with the deliberate long-term planning and expectations, ready to take a leap of faith and live life more spontaneously in the moment.

Without overthinking, I dropped to one knee, pulled out a ring, and proposed. We hadn't been dating long, and I began to feel the nervous tension, wondering if she might say no.

Much to my surprise, she said yes! A rush of emotions flooded me. I was overwhelmed with excitement to have someone by my side, but fear still lingered. I couldn't shake the worry of what the future might hold or the nagging thought that I was pulling her into a life fraught with challenges and uncertainty.

As my time in the P-3C training squadron neared its end, I once again filled out my dream sheet, hoping to remain in Jacksonville. My wish was granted, and I received orders to join the Mad Foxes (VP-5) squadron, which was set to deploy in just under a year. With that timeline in mind, my fiancée and

I began planning for our future and made the spontaneous decision to get married before I joined the team.

We found the perfect house and planned an intimate backyard wedding, surrounded by close friends and family to share this special moment with us. The day turned out to be beautiful, and the weather held out just long enough for a full ceremony and unforgettable photos. After an exciting honeymoon in Savannah, Georgia, we returned to Jacksonville as husband and wife, ready to settle into our new home and embrace the adventure ahead.

From the moment I arrived and met my fellow junior officers, something felt off. I had more than three years of navy experience than all new check-ins, and I'd previously served in another squadron as a junior officer—something that was unheard of. Still, when it came down to it, I was a newcomer, the "new guy," regardless of the higher rank on my shoulder. The gap was undeniable and the contrast jarring. No matter how hard I tried to ignore it, I couldn't shake the feeling that, in the traditional sense, I just didn't quite fit in.

I quickly realized that I needed to take the initiative in conversations, addressing unspoken questions and concerns about my unconventional career path head-on. To bridge the gap between my experience and my new role as the "new guy," or FNG as it is sometimes known, I had to prove that while my path had been different, I was here to be a part of the team.

Simply being part of an operational squadron again was exhilarating. I reflected on my first experience—meeting the team on deployment and how much it had felt like family in those early days. Looking to replicate that same feeling, I walked through the spaces, introduced myself as the newest pilot, and embraced the opportunity to engage in conversation with everyone. I really enjoyed connecting with my new family despite some of the awkward looks and questions about my rank and time in service.

During one of those introductions, I was meeting with one of the department heads when he noticed the difference in my rank compared to the other new check-ins. Curious, he asked about my story. As I walked him through my journey, he casually mentioned that his nephew, who wasn't in the navy, had also been diagnosed with Hodgkin's lymphoma. His nephew had just completed his sixth cycle of chemotherapy and was preparing to begin radiation.

He shared that his nephew was struggling and asked if I would be willing to speak with him, perhaps to offer advice, encouragement, or simply provide the perspective of someone who had been through it. Without hesitation, I agreed. A few days later, his nephew called.

The conversation was both uplifting and unsettling. I was grateful for the opportunity to offer guidance to someone navigating the same difficult path I had traveled, yet his story unearthed a flood of memories that I had long tried to forget. Still, I remained positive and focused on providing encouragement.

We discussed his first few radiation treatments, and I shared my own experience, including my decision to continue with chemotherapy instead. He felt confident in his choice to proceed with radiation, explaining that his body was too weakened to endure more rounds of chemo. It was a meaningful and heartening conversation, and I appreciated connecting with someone on a similar journey. I reassured him that he wasn't alone in this fight and that he could reach out to me anytime.

I received another call after a few weeks, but this time, the news was heartbreaking. While the radiation had been effectively targeting the remaining cancer cells, a fungal infection had developed in his lungs. I did my best to stay positive, offering as much support as I could over the phone, but as I hung up, a deep sense of concern remained. His greatest battle remained ahead of him, and I hoped that he would also be able to find a savior or a defining moment to help him navigate the toughest of times.

Just weeks later, I was devastated to learn that his lungs had filled with fluid one night in an attempt to fight the fungal infection, and he'd passed away. His death made everything feel painfully real again. I couldn't help but reflect on my own journey, questioning the significance of my decision to continue with chemotherapy instead of opting for radiation, not knowing at that time if I was taking control or making a huge mistake. The weight of it all lingered, a sobering reminder of how fragile life truly is and the difficult path I had walked to get here.

My orders to the squadron were for forty-two months. This was a problem because I was behind my year group and the aviation officer career timeline by just over three years after the few months at my first squadron, nine months of chemotherapy, and my mandatory two-year wait. To have any chance of getting back on track with my original timeline to remain both eligible and competitive for promotion to the next rank, I needed to finish this first tour at the same time my year group was finishing their current second tours.

That meant achieving all my qualifications, including instructor pilot, and detaching from the squadron in just thirty months. It quickly became clear that starting from behind didn't guarantee me a spot at the finish line. If I wanted to get back on track for any chance at upward mobility, I had to carve my own path and find a way to leave a full twelve months earlier than expected.

The officers in the wardroom didn't understand my need for an accelerated timeline because it was unheard of that people like me would check into a squadron so far behind their year group. Qualification milestones through examination boards, simulators, and flights were scheduled for each person in the order of their arrival and on a forty-two-month timeline. But I was purposely pushing ahead, deliberately advancing faster than my fellow aviators, because I was on a thirty-month timeline and had to qualify twelve months ahead of schedule. No matter how much I tried to explain my situation, my reasoning created friction within the wardroom. My urgency to accelerate my qualification to depart twelve months earlier than expected was met with skepticism and resistance. The pressures of trying to fit in while pursuing a path for an early departure only fueled their frustration with me.

I was now leapfrogging fellow pilots who had checked in before me, achieving qualification milestones ahead of them. This didn't sit well with many, and they became irritated and, in most cases, infuriated, feeling as if I were taking something away from them. Waiting my turn to advance in my training wasn't an option. To do so would have destroyed any chance for a viable navy career. My next promotion board was set to take place before I even left the squadron, and if I didn't aggressively push forward, I'd never be competitive for advancement.

As we were in the final preparations for our upcoming deployment, I began to feel the weight of being an outsider, viewed as different and separate from the natural order of progression. This was meant to be my triumphant return, my comeback tour, and should have been the most fulfilling chapter of my navy career. Instead, I found myself sprinting toward the finish line, not enjoying the journey and instead desperately racing against time just for a chance to continue my career as a navy pilot.

The day finally arrived when I had to say goodbye to my pregnant wife and board the plane for deployment. She was due in May, and we were scheduled to be deployed until July. There were a couple of terrific things to note about our pregnancy. First, I was relieved to finally stop paying the monthly fees for storing my sperm at the cryobank, validating that chemo hadn't left me sterile, and my cancer-ridden sperm sample was happily destroyed. Second, I took comfort in knowing that the other aviators' wives would be there to provide her with much-needed support while I was gone, especially as she was still adjusting to this exciting new navy lifestyle.

Being on deployment brought back fond memories of my time in Panama and Puerto Rico with my previous squadron. This time, I started deployment in Keflavik, Iceland, then moved on to Rota, Spain, while participating in exercises and missions across France, Germany, Norway, Crete, and Italy. Deployment proved to be the perfect opportunity to study, and I quickly advanced and qualified for the next level of patrol plane pilot (2P). Midway through deployment, our crew was scheduled to fly to Jacksonville in May for a couple of training and readiness simulator events, then continue on to Puerto Rico to finish out the deployment.

My trip to Jacksonville coincided with the due date of our son, but I promised myself not to get too excited since we would only be in town for four days. It was a joyous reunion with my wife, especially since she was much more pregnant than the last time I'd seen her. On the third day, she went into labor, and we rushed to the hospital. After some examinations, the doctor told us it was still too early and sent us home. That night, we walked around the neighborhood, trying everything we could to induce labor. The next morning, I headed to the hangar to begin preflighting our aircraft for our trip to Puerto Rico. About an hour into preflight, the duty officer came aboard the plane and informed me that my wife was in labor at the hospital and being prepped for a C-section. I looked at my crew, and they all smiled and kicked me off the plane. They assured me they'd make arrangements for me to meet them in Puerto Rico in a few days.

Whether it was divine intervention or just pure luck, I was there to witness the birth of our son, nothing short of another miracle. As my wife recovered from the C-section, I spent that first day with our son, savoring all the "dad" moments and reflecting on how incredible it was to be in that moment. A couple of days later, we took our son home, and it was time for me to head to Puerto Rico to finish out the deployment.

Upon arriving in Puerto Rico, a flood of images and memories rushed through my mind, triggered by the familiar sights and scents from my first time there. I couldn't help but reflect on those final, painful days before I'd been medevaced to Bethesda. As I walked to my room, I passed the same clinic where I had spent countless hours waiting for X-ray results. I could almost feel the intense itching again, though I knew it was just a reactive memory. My thoughts, however, were vivid and powerful, making it seem as though I were reliving those moments.

The next two months were spent with my crew, flying missions from Puerto Rico, El Salvador, and the Caribbean island of Curaçao. We bonded as a crew, creating some of the greatest memories together. It was the perfect conclusion to an exciting and, more importantly, fulfilling deployment, one that was finally free from any medical concerns or issues.

Upon our return from deployment, once we were back together as a squadron, the challenges and frustrations in the officer's wardroom persisted. Despite this, I remained on the fast track, which was not popular with everyone. The commanding officer, or "skipper" in aviation, was the one person who truly understood the timing challenges of my navy career. He helped me to accelerate my qualification to patrol plane commander (PPC) and enabled me to become an instructor pilot to remain competitive for advancement. But it wasn't a free pass, and I had to work harder and learn faster than ever before. I fully dedicated myself, and my skipper recognized my effort and progress.

We were on our second multisite deployment, this time to Bahrain and Sigonella, Italy, which gave me the perfect opportunity to build flight hours and gain the necessary instructor experience I needed. I was flying nearly every other day, relishing every moment of being back in the airplane and accumulating valuable experience in the air.

As the end of this deployment drew near, so did the end of my time in the squadron. I learned that I was set to detach early at month thirty, an accomplishment I had been working toward for so long. In the final days, I walked into my skipper's office and thanked him for understanding my situation, for not judging me because of my past, and for giving me the opportunity to prove myself through my drive, resilience, and performance. If not for his decisions and the chances he took on me, my navy career would have ended before it truly began. His support became the turning point I desperately needed.

CHAPTER VII

After navigating the complexities of an accelerated timeline in VP-5, I successfully met the key milestones necessary to further advance in my career. This led to me receiving orders to San Diego, California, where I would soon report to USS *Nimitz* (CVN-68) for our next adventure. Typically, after completing a tour with a deploying squadron, I would be assigned to a shore command. However, the three years I spent undergoing chemotherapy and attending Naval Postgraduate School had effectively become my shore tour. As a result, and as a necessity to catch back up to my original timeline, I received orders from one deploying tour right into another.

Meanwhile, back in Jacksonville, my wife, pregnant with our second child, was managing the logistics of our upcoming household move, all while I remained deployed in Italy. We were thrilled to receive orders to San Diego, bringing us back to her home state of California. For her, it meant returning closer to family and familiar roots; for me, it marked the beginning of a new and welcomed chapter.

Still in Italy, I checked out of VP-5 and boarded a commercial flight back to Jacksonville, where my wife met me after handling the bulk of the cross-country move herself. She had already shipped our household goods and second vehicle to San Diego, then flown back just to meet me. From there, we set off together, another cross-country drive filled with anticipation and exhaustion, arriving in San Diego in March 2005. After a few days of unpacking and settling in, I began several months of classroom training in preparation for my upcoming assignment aboard the ship. By late June, my training was complete, and I was left waiting for orders to determine when and where I would join the ship, which was already deployed. With our second child due in July, the uncertainty was heavy. I knew my departure was imminent and feared I would miss the birth. When orders finally arrived, I was scheduled to depart on July 15 via commercial flight to meet the ship at its next port call.

Once again, whether by divine intervention or sheer luck, the doctor scheduled a C-section for July 8. I was incredibly fortunate to be there for the birth of our daughter, cherishing that first day with her, soaking in every "dad" moment, holding her tiny hand, and reflecting once again on the sheer miracle of it all while my wife recovered from surgery. With the odds and timeline stacked against me, being present for the births of both of our children felt like an immeasurable gift, one that so many service members miss while sacrificing personal moments for professional commitments.

After spending a few precious days with my growing family, I boarded a commercial flight to Bahrain to join the ship. Stepping aboard, I found myself in a completely new and disorienting environment: a labyrinth of narrow hallways, stepladders, and heavy hatches. Fortunately, my new shipmates welcomed me with patience and camaraderie, guiding me through the chaos. They led me to my stateroom, where I unpacked a few belongings, then walked me to a few select areas to meet the team and become oriented. I spent the remainder of that day learning to navigate the ship and how to get to my assigned workspace, where I would begin the next day.

Even though I wasn't flying, this assignment offered a refreshing change and a valuable opportunity to immerse myself in a fast-paced operational environment. The deployment was filled with countless opportunities to learn, grow, and apply new skills, and I made steady progress toward key qualifications and milestones that were critical steps to getting my career back on track. I remained concerned that, despite my best efforts, I would need to perform at the highest level to make up for lost time and stay competitive to earn advancement to the next rank.

While much of our time was spent at sea, we were fortunate to enjoy port visits in Bahrain, Dubai, and Australia, making the most of every opportunity to explore new and exciting places. But life aboard the ship was relentless. The ship never sleeps, and there's always work to be done around the clock. I held multiple roles and stood various watches at all hours of the day. Depending upon the assignment, I might catch a glimpse of the outside world, but more often, especially in those early days, I remained deep within the ship's interior, establishing a routine that was both demanding and deeply rewarding.

In just a few months, I was promoted to a new role and began training as officer of the deck (underway), a position where I would soon be responsible for the safe navigation and conduct of the ship while at sea. This position offered a welcome shift, literally giving me a view of the outside world each day, along with a bird's eye view and front-row seat to launching and recovering aircraft operations. By then, I had settled into a steady routine, and my time on the bridge of the ship, often during late-night watches, became a quiet refuge. Those hours were calm and introspective, a rare moment of peace that stood in stark contrast to the constant motion and noise that filled the rest of the ship.

By the time we returned from deployment, I had earned all the necessary skills and qualifications available to me, becoming proficient in ship handling and finally mastering exactly which galley served the best meals at each time of day. In the months that followed, we cycled in and out of port for various exercises and training events, but there was still time to reconnect with family. It was incredible to see how much the kids had grown in my absence, proof of how quickly time moves while underway.

While I was unexpectedly enjoying this assignment onboard a ship and not flying an aircraft, my desire to return to aviation was reignited. I was thrilled to learn I had been promoted to lieutenant commander (O-4) and selected for department head, two accomplishments that had felt out of reach just a short time ago. As much as I had grown to appreciate my time at sea, I was more than ready to return to the cockpit.

It had been five years since my last chemotherapy treatment, and I was finally beginning to understand my new normal. The constant anxiety over every little chest pain had faded, and while the lasting effects of chemotherapy on my body were well-known to me, they remained life-altering in ways both seen and unseen. Much of the permanent damage was internal, revealed through routine blood work, X-rays, and echocardiograms, along with the persistent fog of chemo brain. Yet, the physical impairments were still very real and ongoing.

The same chemotherapy that had disintegrated the veins in my arms had also disrupted blood flow and nerve function throughout my body. In colder temperatures, my fingers and toes would numb, turning first pale white, then purple. My lungs no longer had the same endurance or strength during exercise, reduced by chemotherapy's toxicity. While these effects were not incapacitating, their long-term impacts remained uncertain yet undeniably harmful. And in the back of my mind, there was always a quiet voice wondering what else might arise or, worse, what might possibly return. Life seemed to be on track, yet every day carried a sense of unease and anxiety, as if something unknown might be lurking ahead.

Despite the challenges of being away from aviation and flying, my time on the ship ended up offering its own kind of purpose and growth. The constant pressures of medical waivers and the frantic race to reestablish myself on the aviation officer career timeline were finally behind me. While I had barely met the navy's promotion requirements in both flight hours and time, I was finally back on track with a renewed opportunity to excel and continue advancing in my career.

As my time aboard the ship came to a close, the department head assignments were published, and I learned that my next tour would be with the Grey Knights (VP-46) squadron in Whidbey Island, Washington. Eager to return to aviation, I was equally excited about the opportunity to relocate my family to a new place, one we hadn't yet explored. It felt like a fresh chapter—the promise of discovering the area while watching the kids grow. And perhaps most of all, we were relieved at the thought that we wouldn't have to drive cross-country again, at least not for now.

Our move from San Diego to Whidbey Island was more complex than our first relocation together, from Monterey to Jacksonville, when we'd simply packed our belongings into a truck and driven across the country. Now, with a family of four, the logistics were more complicated, and the kids seemed to have more furniture and belongings than we did. For the first time since we'd been together, we had to drive separately, each of us in our own vehicle, traveling in tandem up the coast. While this might not seem significant on the surface, as I drove alone, I couldn't help but reflect on my lonely cross-country drive after chemotherapy and the journey I had navigated up to this moment.

Once we arrived and settled into our new home, I boarded a commercial flight to Jacksonville for refresher training in the P-3C aircraft, having been away from aviation for several years. Now that I was a department head, the training was much shorter, only three months. While I was sad to be away from my family, the separation was brief, and it provided me the opportunity to reconnect with my bike racing team. I rode with them every day, knowing that racing opportunities would be limited in Whidbey Island and that I would soon be deploying again, just a few months after checking in to the squadron.

With training complete, my return to Whidbey Island was met with three smiling faces and a young daughter who was now much more active, running around the house. On my first real chance to explore the area, I found a local bike group to ride with on occasion. While they were not as fast as my team in Jacksonville, the change in terrain was a welcome challenge. The mountainous routes were a stark contrast to the flat courses I had been accustomed to in Florida, and I found that I had plenty to learn about riding in these new conditions.

I was filled with excitement the day I walked into the hangar of my new squadron, anticipating a warm welcome reminiscent of the one I had received from my very first squadron, long before chemotherapy. However, when I arrived, I was immediately met with familiar disapproving comments and questions about my career path, questions I had already addressed previously and thought I had long since put behind me. This time, however, the scrutiny had shifted. Instead of being judged for my difference in rank, I was now criticized for straying from the traditional officer career path and for missing what others deemed a crucial shore tour, something cancer had taken from me. My worth was immediately minimized to a single piece of paper outlining my career path and flight hours, without giving me the opportunity to prove myself through performance in an airplane or assigned ground duties. In that moment, my unconventional journey became the defining measure of my character, and not in a positive way. All the experiences, sacrifices, and strengths that had shaped me were reduced to a single, unforgiving label.

It was a harsh realization that, from this point forward, my unconventional navy journey would not always be met with acceptance or recognition. The naval aviation community is grounded in well-established standards and is accustomed to officers progressing along a very traditional, clearly defined career path. With delays caused by cancer and past assignments to the Naval Historical Center and the Naval Postgraduate School on my record, I knew the scrutiny was far from over.

Questions and skepticism would continue to cast a shadow over everything I had worked and stood for. I would have to prove myself in ways that other aviators never had to.

This tour had begun with a discouraging and negative start to what had promised to be another exciting return to aviation. However, once we deployed overseas and the squadron split among different deployment sites, I redirected my focus and attention to flying operational missions with my crew and instructing junior pilots through their career milestones. While flying missions was fulfilling and provided invaluable experience, the lingering sense of being ostracized for not fitting the traditional career path remained, and my future, at best, felt uncertain.

Drawing from the challenges of my past and approaching the situation with cautious optimism, I poured everything I had into the job, all while bracing for the worst. I had navigated an impossible journey, and despite the negativity and obstacles of my unconventional career path, I had reached a point where I could truly take pride in my achievements as a navy pilot. More importantly, I was incredibly proud of overcoming cancer and enduring hardships that no one should have to face in a lifetime. In that moment, I realized that, regardless of the outcome of this tour, I would be at peace, knowing I had given it my all, even in the face of adversity.

Meanwhile, the Northwest region proved to be an exciting place for the family. The kids were still young, but they were just old enough to enjoy small family trips that included skiing in Whistler, cruises to Canada and Alaska, camping at state parks, and ferry rides to Seattle for fun and adventure. It was truly a memorable time, and even during the toughest moments, it gave me a sense of hope. I rarely thought about my lung anymore, and even now, the negative effects from chemotherapy felt like old news and were just part of my new normal.

After returning from deployment, I entered the final six months of my tour at the command. In an unexpected turn of events, I was assigned as the maintenance officer for my last role. It was the very challenge I had been seeking, a chance to prove myself when I needed it the most. With the dissolution of the Combined Maintenance Organization, which had previously serviced all P-3C aircraft on the base, each squadron was now responsible for managing the maintenance of their own aircraft. As the maintenance officer, I was tasked with rebuilding the entire maintenance department from the ground up. It wasn't just about managing day-to-day operations but also about crafting a new foundation from scratch, navigating complexities, and pushing my limits in ways I hadn't anticipated.

This was my opportunity to apply everything I had learned from my unconventional journey, and I felt confident that I was the right person for the job. Our first challenge was reintegrating over two hundred maintenance personnel back into the squadron, a complex administrative feat in itself. Once we successfully completed that, we turned our focus to rebuilding each maintenance division, creating tailored programs, and rewriting instructions and notices to meet our specific needs. With a fully operational maintenance team in place, we faced the final hurdle: preparing for our certification assessment. This was the crucial step before we could assume full responsibility for maintaining our assigned aircraft, and it was a make-or-break moment for both the squadron and me.

Having spent much of my career facing challenges and forging my path independently, I felt ready to take on the task of uniting over two hundred maintainers, not just to perform their technical duties but also to cultivate a strong, cohesive team. This role embodied the lessons my unique, unconventional career path had taught me. Naturally, the journey wasn't without challenges, including some confrontational moments that demanded careful leadership and diplomacy. But in the end, the reestablishment of the maintenance department was a complete success. The team we built emerged stronger, more unified, and fully prepared to take on the mission ahead.

After a difficult and confrontational start, I took immense pride in what I had accomplished despite the obstacles I had faced. As my tour came to a close, I received orders for my next assignment as an executive assistant to the assistant secretary of defense at the Pentagon. For the first time in years, I allowed myself to truly savor this professional milestone, not just for the recognition but also for what it symbolized. My strength and resilience had carried me through some of the toughest challenges in life, and ultimately, they proved to be the most meaningful reward.

Ready for another adventure—and another cross-country trip—we packed up the family in one vehicle and shipped the other as we set off for Washington, DC, on Thanksgiving Day, 2009. Whether by coincidence or just sheer happenstance, I couldn't help but reflect on another Thanksgiving Day, fourteen years earlier in 1995. Back then, I had sat alone in the suffocating silence of my college apartment, uncertain of what the future held, with staples holding my lung together and "sticky glue" securing it to my chest cavity. Now, laughter and music filled the car as my family sat beside me, smiling and singing along to the radio, their warmth replacing the solitude I had once known. The contrast was striking, a powerful reminder of how far I had come.

The Pentagon was exactly what you would expect: a relentless, fast-paced environment where military personnel reported to their respective jobs, worked long hours, then moved on to their next career milestone, only to be replaced by the next military person in line. Despite the intensity, all the hard work supported the Department of Defense at the highest levels, offering remarkable exposure and experience to my career. At times, the job felt like a giant meat grinder, but in the end, it was both positive and fulfilling.

I'd been in this role just under a year when I learned that I had been promoted to commander (O-5) and reached the career milestone of being considered for aviation command. With only a nominal 50 percent selection rate among eligible officers, I knew the competition would be fierce. The other candidates were highly experienced, well-regarded, and accomplished within the aviation community. I had never been a conventional fit, often seen as different, and at times, that difference was viewed unfavorably.

To improve my chances for what felt like an insurmountable barrier, I submitted a letter of medical explanation to the selection board. In it, I outlined my Hodgkin's lymphoma diagnosis, the challenges I had overcome, my subsequent achievements, and the accelerated career path I had navigated. I hoped that by providing that context, the board would gain a deeper understanding of my journey and the resilience that had shaped my record and performance, thus seeing beyond the traditional measure of what made a candidate worthy of selection.

The Pentagon was the first navy assignment where I had the unique opportunity to work primarily with non-military personnel across the Department of Defense and various other federal government agencies. I had the privilege of serving under the assistant secretary of defense for global strategic affairs, an exceptional leader and the most remarkable person whose guidance and vision left a lasting imprint on my career. This assignment exposed me to a diverse range of leadership styles across the government, shaping my perspective and playing a pivotal role in defining the kind of leader I aspired to become.

This role pushed me far beyond my comfort zone in aviation and navy operations. I found myself providing military insight while collaborating with a team to develop and shape policies on nuclear forces, missile defense, countering weapons of mass destruction, cybersecurity, and space policy. As executive assistant, I frequently accompanied the assistant secretary on overseas trips to London, Paris, and, most often, NATO Headquarters in Brussels. It was an invaluable opportunity that taught me how to work effectively within a team where authority wasn't defined by a visible rank device but by expertise, collaboration, and shared responsibility.

My family truly enjoyed living in the Washington, DC, area. While there was always something to do, our best memories came from the simple days at home, especially during the winter, when our front yard transformed into the perfect sledding hill. The Snowmageddon of 2010 brought an entire week of pure excitement for the kids, who had only ever experienced brief encounters with snow on our trips to Whistler, Canada.

The area around the Pentagon provided the perfect opportunity for me to rediscover my passion for running. Each day, I took advantage of my lunch hour to explore the surrounding area, pounding the pavement and experiencing some of the most amazing runs of my life. During cherry blossom season, the route around Hains Point transformed into a magnificent corridor of pink and white, a natural masterpiece that simply couldn't be replicated. When I craved a break from the pavement, Theodore Roosevelt Island, an 88.5-acre national park nestled in the middle of the Potomac River, offered shaded trails and a tree canopy, making it an ideal retreat on those hot summer days. When I was in the mood for a more moderate-paced, longer run, I would venture to the National Mall and loop around the Capitol, enjoying a smooth and scenic ten-mile route.

Invigorated by the opportunities in the area and with more free time than during my previous aviation tours, I dove back into triathlons. I joined a local cycling group, which provided the support and competition I desperately needed to improve both my strength and racing technique. My race times were comparable to those from my days in Monterey, and though I had regained significant strength, I could feel that my lung efficiency was the limiting factor in further improvement. The damage from the collapse and toxicity of chemotherapy had left a lasting toll on my lungs, but I pushed through it, continuing to build my endurance and strength.

After several years of intense training and racing, my Achilles tendons finally had enough. They became inflamed and painfully sore to the touch. While they hadn't ruptured, the chronic pain from microscopic tears brought sharp, aching discomfort and swelling, likely caused by overuse and years of wearing flight boots. Bordering on being a tragedy, this marked a significant turning point for me, one where I lost my go-to outlet for stress relief. No longer could I just slip on a pair of running shoes and run freely to clear my mind and improve my fitness. While I could still manage much shorter distances and a slower pace, I would never again find that enduring runner's high or that authentic feeling of gliding over the ground during the perfect run.

Then, on no particular day, I was sitting at my desk when the phone rang. It was a friend delivering the joyous news that I had been selected for aviation command. For a brief moment, absolute shock eclipsed my excitement, but as reality sank in, I was overwhelmed with gratitude and relief. I had agonized over whether my letter to the board had effectively conveyed my achievements despite the obstacles I had faced. I feared they might overlook my journey, dismissing my unconventional career path in favor of more traditional candidates. But in that moment, for the first time in my career, I felt truly seen, not for the challenges I had endured but for the accomplishments I had achieved. It was a milestone unlike any other, a powerful validation of the perseverance and determination that had defined my entire career journey.

Surviving cancer had been one of the greatest challenges of my life, but it had also forged a foundation of strength, shaping me into a more resilient leader, listener, and problem solver. Aviation command was no different, and I would need to lean upon that resilience to navigate its challenges and demands.

But I was ready, confident that my journey had prepared me for this very moment.

Our time in Washington, DC, had come to an end, and while my family had really enjoyed our time there, we were ready to get back to aviation. When the official assignment list was published, I found that I'd been assigned to the Fighting Tigers (VP-8) squadron in Jacksonville, Florida. Excited about not having to drive cross-country again, we packed up our belongings and headed south.

Reporting as the executive officer, I spent the year getting to know every sailor by name, fully immersing myself in the heartbeat of the squadron's operations. My skipper wasn't just my boss—he was a true friend, a person of the finest kind. He embodied integrity in ways that left an indelible mark on every member, setting the standard for leadership and character. He became my teacher, showing me what it truly meant to lead with honor, purpose, and vision. In return, I took on all the behind-the-scenes tasks and administrative labor with unwavering commitment, ensuring he could enjoy being the face of the squadron and leading with the clarity and focus that only a great skipper can.

As the senior pilot, I was entrusted with the responsibility of training junior pilots and shaping them into leaders, teammates, and, most importantly, skilled technical and tactical aviators. I was a tough teacher, pushing them beyond their comfort zones with challenging training scenarios designed to prepare them for the real pressures of flying missions with their crews. While my approach wasn't always appreciated, I was proud to have watched each of them grow into the best versions of themselves, fully prepared for whatever lay ahead, both in the air and in life.

The squadron had become a second family. As we readied ourselves for the upcoming deployment, I made it a priority to check in with the sailors, especially the first-time deployers, to help ease their concerns. With our two deployment sites separated by over 8,500 miles, I flew with each aircrew to ensure they were fully trained and prepared for the missions ahead. It was rewarding to see that our rigorous training program had fostered the leadership necessary in each aircrew to address any challenges that might arise during deployment. After spending time with friends and family for Thanksgiving, we were out the door on deployment just a few weeks later.

After a few months of deployment and a year as executive officer, I was ready to take the helm and command the Fighting Tigers. In March 2014, while still deployed, we held a small change of command ceremony, an intimate moment amid the operational grind. I said goodbye to my friend and skipper as he departed for his next adventure and, in the same breath, welcomed another close friend to VP-8 as my new executive officer. It was a quiet but powerful passing of the torch just before we snapped back to the mission, with four more months of deployment ahead.

This was the pinnacle achievement of my aviation career. Not just because I had become the sixty-sixth commanding officer or held the coveted title of skipper but also because I was finally in a position to give back. To guide, mentor, and support others through their own personal and professional challenges. I came to realize that it wasn't the flying itself I had been chasing all these years; it was this moment. This opportunity. Right here, right now. To lead with purpose and to be there for others the way I had needed someone to be there for me in the past.

Together, the Fighting Tigers delivered exceptional performance across every metric, earning the top two most prestigious awards and achieving the highest retention rate among all the squadrons. We also set a new standard for excellence with what the training and assessment team called the "best ever" transition from the P-3C to the P-8A aircraft. While those accolades were meaningful, my deepest pride didn't come from the trophies or formal recognition—it came from the team itself. Their relentless dedication, toughness, and ability to meet every challenge with unwavering positivity and pride were the true measure of our success.

Despite that success, I continued to face daunting adversity from the aviation leaders above me, especially during performance evaluations. My nontraditional career path and cancer history weren't just footnotes; they were seen as permanent personal flaws and unshakeable defects, like a tattoo across my forehead that I never chose but that everyone could see. I was judged instantly and almost entirely by my past, with little regard or comment given to my actual performance or achievements. Still, our squadron went on to set the "gold standard," as described by those same leaders, proving that resilience, hard work, and commitment—not a person's career path—drive results.

My time in command of VP-8 flew by, and before long, the end was approaching. As we began preparing for the upcoming change of command ceremony, I knew I had to choose a guest speaker, someone who embodied integrity, strength, and honor. The significance of the moment left no doubt in my mind. Without hesitation, I asked my former skipper from VP-5. He was the one person who truly understood the journey I had taken, the timeline I had navigated, and the challenges I had overcome. Nearly a decade earlier, he had played a pivotal role in accelerating my timeline during my junior officer tour, making it possible for me to stand there, in that moment, as a skipper myself.

The change of command ceremony was a powerful lesson in perspective. For the sailors and aviators, it was a formal military tradition marking the official transfer of authority and responsibility from one officer to another. But as I stood on that stage delivering my farewell remarks, I saw more than a ceremony. I saw the faces of my incredible team and, behind them, the P-3C and P-8A aircraft lined up together, symbols of the excellence and success we had redefined together. It was an honor to have led them to that moment and a profound reminder of how far I had come on an unconventional journey that had shaped not only my path but also the leader I had become.

CHAPTER VIII

A s I reflect on my journey, I see a life defined by resilience, transformation, and an unwavering drive to push forward despite the obstacles that stood in my way. My time in the navy was marked by extraordinary highs and unyielding lows, ranging from the exhilaration of earning my pilot wings to the devastation of an unexpected medical diagnosis. Each experience, whether in the airplane, the hospital, or in a leadership role, has shaped the person I have become.

My early years as a naval aviator were everything I had dreamed of, from flying missions with an elite team to embracing the challenges of deployment to feeling the thrill of being a part of something greater than myself. But life had a different plan. A battle with Hodgkin's lymphoma forced me to step away from flying, leading to years of uncertainty, frustration, and the fear that my career and, at one point, my life, might be over. Yet, my return to flying, though delayed and fraught with challenges, rekindled my passion and reaffirmed my resilience.

As my career progressed from one squadron to the next and eventually into a command role and beyond, I faced new trials and unpredicted obstacles, balancing leadership, operational demands, and the weight of personal expectations. Each assignment offered opportunities to learn, grow, and redefine what success meant to me, not to the person signing my performance evaluation. My career did not always follow the traditional path, but it was uniquely mine, filled with lessons and insights that reached far beyond aviation.

The navy provided me more than just a career; it offered me a family, a sense of purpose, and experiences that will forever shape my perspective. As this chapter closes and I step into the next phase of my life, I do so with the same spirit that carried me through the years: the drive to keep moving forward, embrace new challenges, and continue learning. The road ahead may be uncertain, but if my past has taught me anything, it's that I am ready for whatever comes next.

CONCLUSION

There was a time when I believed life followed a neat, predictable path with checkpoints and milestones laid out like a flight plan, leading to some picture-perfect destination. But life doesn't work that way. It throws storms in your path, forces you into uncharted airspace, and sometimes rips away the very things you thought defined you. The key is learning to navigate the turbulence, to stop chasing an illusion of an unattainable perfect future, and to find joy in the moment you're in.

I've learned that strength isn't just about survival. It's about refusing to be defined by anything or anyone but yourself. I've charted a course that defied expectations, and if that made my journey seem unconventional, perhaps the problem lies with the expectations, not with me. None of us fit into a perfect template, and none of us follow the same flight path. And that's exactly the point.

If you ever find yourself on the receiving end of life's worst news, or if the ground drops out from beneath you and someone tells you, "It's going to be okay," know that it's perfectly acceptable to reject that notion. Because sometimes, it won't be okay, and we both know it. Instead, surround yourself with the ones who show up, the ones who stand beside you in the uncertainty, the ones who hand you a bad reality TV show and say, "Let's get through this together." That's what matters. That's what carries you through.

And when you do make it through, because one way or another, you will, don't let the battle, the scars, or anyone else's expectations define you. You are the one who decides who you are. You get to choose what comes next.

Now go—be fearless, stay true, and most importantly, keep on keepin' on.

ACKNOWLEDGMENTS

To write a book like this is to dig up the past, stitch together memories, and occasionally wonder why you ever saved that one embarrassing story. But here we are—and I wouldn't have made it here alone.

First and foremost, to my family—thank you for being the steady ground beneath all my takeoffs and crash landings. To my wife, whose patience is legendary and whose love is the quiet strength behind every chapter—thank you for holding me up when I wasn't sure which way was up. To my kids—you are the reason I fight harder, laugh louder, and sometimes hide snacks in the garage.

To my dad for giving me the kind of childhood that could fill a book—and then some. You gave me direction, toughness, and the kind of love that never needed words to be understood.

To my extended family—thank you for the memories on the farm, the laughter, the chores, and the endless supply of life lessons (and colorful language) that have shaped who I am. You gave me more than just stories—you gave me the grit and humor to survive them.

To my running shoes—thanks for carrying me through the chaos of life. Every step helped clear my head and rebuild my spirit. And to the eighties hair metal bands that blasted from my Walkman straight into my soul. You didn't just deliver music—you provided therapy, volume, and the inspiration behind my truly questionable fashion choices.

And finally, to the select few who believed in me when I wasn't sure I could believe in myself—who were there at my lowest and never let go—thank you. You didn't just lift me up. You helped me soar. This story is as much yours as it is mine.

ABOUT THE AUTHOR

Derek Adametz was born and raised outside of Madison in the beautiful state of Wisconsin. A retired navy captain and former naval aviator, Derek's career—and life—shifted course after a cancer diagnosis. Through years of military service and battles fought both in the air and on the ground, he discovered a deeper story worth telling. His writing explores themes of resilience, transformation, and quiet perseverance. He now lives in Chesapeake, Virginia, where he continues to write and reflect on the journey that shaped him. *Unbreakable Wings* is his debut memoir.

www.ingramcontent.com/pod-product-compliance
Lightning Source LLC
Chambersburg PA
CBHW021639120626
46545CB00002B/620